BEADED WRIST WARMERS FROM LITHUANIA

Irena Felomena Juškienė

Beaded Wrist Warmers from Lithuania
63 Knitting Patterns in the Baltic Tradition

Trafalgar Square
North Pomfret, Vermont

First published in the United States of America in 2018 by
Trafalgar Square Books
North Pomfret, Vermont 05053

Originally published in Lithuanian as *Riešinės*.

Copyright © 2008 Irena Felomena Juškienė
English translation © 2018 Trafalgar Square Books

All rights reserved. No part of this book may be reproduced, by any means, without written permission of the publisher, except by a reviewer quoting brief excerpts for a review in a magazine or newspaper or on a website.

ISBN: 978-1-57076-904-7

Library of Congress Control Number: 2018954578

This book includes additional photographs courtesy of Zita Baniulaitė and Sigita Jurkonienė.
Summary: Laimutė Zabulienė, Gražina Vasiliauskienė, Liudmila Plytnikienė
Charts for wrist warmers: Giedrė Brazytė, Živilė Kazlienė, Jūratė Veteikytė
Photography: Skaidrius Juška, Jūratė Veteikytė
Interior layout: Jūratė Veteikytė
Stylist: Marija Razmukaitė
Translation into English: Donna Druchunas
Cover design: RM Didier

Printed in China
10 9 8 7 6 5 4 3 2 1

Contents

Introduction	6
Wrist Warmers	9
What are "Riešinės"?	9
A Short History of Wrist Warmers in Lithuania and Europe	10
Lithuanian Wrist Warmer Styles	13
Knitting Beaded Wrist Warmers	17
Beading Cheats and Knitted Samples	22
Appendix 1: Other Wool Wrist Warmers in Museum Collections	150
Appendix 2: Linen and Cotton Fingerless Gloves	172
Contributors	176
Stories from Contributors	177
Sources	184
References	185
Abbreviations	186
List of Wrist Warmers Organized by Ethnographic Region	186
Translator's Notes	194
Finishing Techniques	196
Yarn Information	199

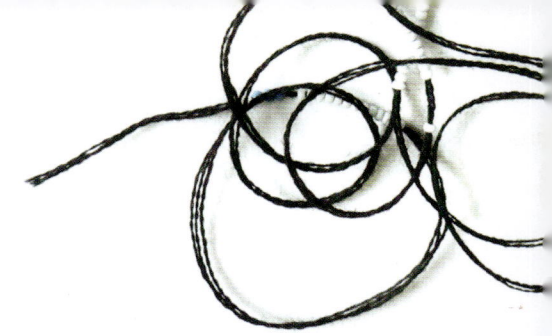

Introduction

Lithuanians cherish our culture. We often say that Lithuanian and Baltic culture is ancient, important, interesting, and nourishing to the soul, just like our language and our treasured woven sash patterns. Our cherished artifacts serve as a valuable lens through which to view our traditions, and we want to share our cultural treasures with people from other parts of the world. Simple objects can be appreciated by researchers and collectors from anywhere and everywhere. I believe and hope that this book, with my thorough presentation of one aspect of Lithuanian ethnographic culture, will expand the circle of appreciation.

This work is not a scientific catalog or publication. It is the result of my leisure activities, and I believe the material here will be fascinating to other people interested in ethnographic heritage.

I have been interested in studying and knitting wrist warmers for over 20 years. This is the story of how I "got to know" them:

When the folk ensemble "Ula," of which I was a member, was founded, the group needed costumes to wear when performing. At that time, the leader of the ensemble, Aldona Ragevičienė, taught us not only songs and dances, but also about the traditional clothing that comprises the Lithuanian national folk costume. I remember visiting the exhibits in the Lithuanian National Museum (formerly the History and Ethnography Museum), where ethnographer Stasys Bernotienė showed us wrist warmers, which we had never seen before. She explained how and when they were worn. Then Aldona Ragevičienė said, "I don't understand why Lithuanian girls don't wear wrist warmers any more. After all, they do parade around like princesses." These words inspired me to take a deeper look at traditional wrist warmers, to knit reproductions of the examples that were still in the museums, and to try to create a pattern book with practical tips for knitters.

At the end of the nineteenth century and the beginning of the twentieth century, women and men, adults and children, all wore wrist warmers. These knitted cuffs were worn both because they were practical for keeping warm, and because they were beautiful. At the time, wrist warmers were very popular, but they fell out of fashion in the middle of the twentieth century. Today, they've been reborn as popular, decorative, gorgeous accessories. According to one doctor in Vilnius, "Every self-respecting woman should wear wrist warmers. They are both beautiful and warm."

In this book, I've tried to showcase all of the remaining antique wrist warmers in Lithuanian museums, as well as those in private collections. Most are in good shape. Over time, however, some began to deteriorate and fall apart, while others, perhaps those that were worn less often, are still in excellent condition. In the main sections of this book, I've focused on the beaded wrist warmers that are in museums, private collections, and vintage publications. I've also included knitting techniques and illustrations, along with instructions and charts for making the wrist warmers shown in the photographs. Wrist warmers that were made without beads are included in a separate appendix, organized by the Lithuanian ethnographic region where they were made. And finally, I've included a selection of knitted and crocheted fingerless gloves that are made from cotton and linen. I hope you will find all of these sections interesting.

I sincerely thank all those who contributed to the publication of this book from the Ministry of Culture. For moral and nongovernmental support, I thank: the Birzai Sėla Museum, the Kaišiadorys Museum, Lithuanian Art Museum, the Open-Air Museum of Lithuania, Lithuanian National Museum, Marijampolė Regional Museum, Mažeikiai Museum, M. K. Čiurlionis National Museum of Art, the Panevėžys Regional Museum, the Šiauliai Aušra Museum, Antanas and Anastasia Tamošaitis Gallery "Židinys," the Upyna

Folk Crafts Museum (Šilalė district), Vilkaviškis Regional Museum, Samogitian Alka Museum, and the Palanga Traditional Textile Training Center for giving me access to their preserved examples of wrist warmers and for sharing their knowledge with me. For advice, I thank ethnographer Dalia Bernotaitė-Beliauskienė, ethnic culture specialist Irena Seliukaitė, and Marija Razmukaitė, Doctor of Linguistics.

For information about examples of wrist warmers from neighboring countries and other areas, I thank Ulia Gintnerė, Astra Dzervė, Sviatlana Klepikava, Igoris Tonurist, and Raimonda Narbutienė.

I sincerely thank all of the knitters of the past and their family members, some of whom have shared their loving memories, others of whom shared their own personal collection of knitting with me, and all of today's knitters who helped to popularize wrist warmers once again. Just like the wrist warmers that survived and were miraculously preserved in our museums were worn every day, today beautifully detailed accessories are being worn by Lithuanians not only as part of the national costume for folk ensembles and other groups, but also with every-day and fashionable clothes at home and at work.

Finally, I would like to thank Donna Druchunas, who helped me start the process of getting this book published in the United States, and who translated the text. I am very pleased that the book will reach more readers.

I dedicate this work to my grandmother Veronika Žiemytė-Deveikienė (1883-1945), who came from the village of Antalamėstė, Saldutiškis District, Utenas County. She was a master weaver, who had hope chests full to overflowing with her handiwork to bring as a dowry when she got married.

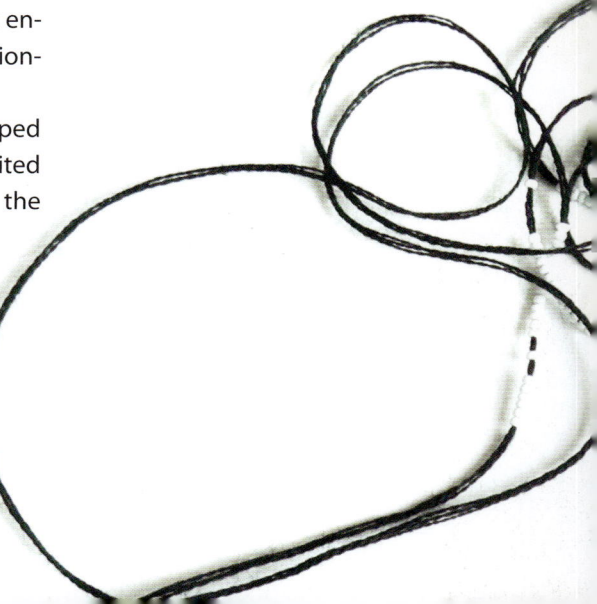

WRIST WARMERS

What are "Riešinės"?

The largest Lithuanian dictionary[1] defines "*riešinė*" (wrist warmer)[2] as:
1. a glove with a long patterned cuff (from the town of Tauragnai)
2. a knitted cuff worn on the wrist

The second meaning is more common.

Marytė Jankauskaitė-Čižienė remembers that in the village of Paalksnės, Moletai District, knitted tubes worn on the wrist were also called *rankogaliai* (cuffs), "because they were around the wrists like a sleeve cuff." In Joniškis "we only called them *riešinės* (wrist warmers) and had no other words for them," recalled Genovaitė Jovaišaitė–Povilaitienė.

In the five ethnographic regions of Lithuania, many different words were used to describe wrist warmers, just as in English they might be called wristers, mitts, fingerless gloves, cuffs, sweatbands, wristbands, wristlets, bangles, armlets, armbands, or even bracelets.

Stories from knitters and their family members make it clear that wrist warmers were meant to be worn every day, both indoors and outdoors. Men and women wore wrist warmers all the time, especially in cold weather and while working in the fields and in the forests. At the time, shirts and blouses had wide sleeves, and wrist warmers were used to gather the sleeve in at the cuff so it would be warmer while working or driving horse-drawn carts. Wrist warmers were especially useful for children because they outgrew their shirt sleeves so quickly. Our great-grandparents never took off their

---

[1] *Lietuvių kalbos žodynas*, Volume 11, p. 575.
[2] The noun is defined and contains the same root in all parts of speech: *ríešinė, ríešinės, ríešinei, ríešinę, su ríešine, ríešinėje; ríešines, ríešinių, ríešinėms, ríešines, su ríešinėm (is), ríešinėse.*

wrist warmers, neither in winter nor in summer!

Wrist warmers weren't only worn for working outdoors. They were also worn to keep warm when sitting indoors, and for dressing up, when it was important for their highly-decorated edges to peek out and be visible from under your coat sleeves.

A Short History of Wrist Warmers in Lithuania and Europe

In the nineteenth and twentieth centuries, in Europe, especially in Scandinavia, wrist warmers knit from wool yarn were widespread. They were worn in Latvia, Estonia, Belarus, Poland, the Czech Republic, Finland, Scandinavia, Germany, and England. Some Nordic countries, such as Iceland and Greenland, have kept up the tradition of wearing wrist warmers. The Danish National Museum displays wrist warmers in an exhibit on the national costumes of Greenland. And knitters in America make wrist warmers with musk-ox wool that are inspired by traditional Alaskan Inuit designs[3].

On the Shetland Islands (the Scottish archipelago between Great Britain and Norway), people often wore wrist warmers in the nineteenth and early twentieth centuries[4]. Later, fingerless gloves became more popular. As early as the sixteenth century, the inhabitants of the Shetland Islands traded extensively traded with Baltic and Scandinavian countries, as well as with Germany and the Neth-

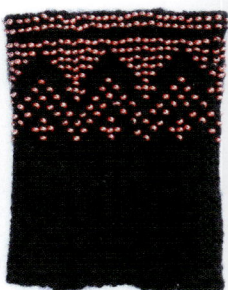

---

[3] Druchunas, Donna. *Arctic Lace: Knitting Projects and Stories Inspired by Alaska's Native Knitters.* // Nomad press. Fort Collins, Colorado, 2006, page 122.

[4] Carol Rasmussen Noble. *Knitting Fair Isle Mittens & Gloves: 40 Great-Looking Designs.*// Lark Books, Asheville, North Carolina, 2002, page 11.

[5] Kirsten Rømcke and Nina Granlund Sæther. *Perler på pulsen.* // Norges Hus idslag. 2004, page 9. Example of wrist warmer from of Raimonda Narbutienė's personal collection.

[6] Elzbieta Piskorz–Branekova. *Polskie stroje ludowe.* // Sport i Turystyka–Muza Sa. // Warszawa. 2005, pages 36–41.

erlands. In this way, knitting designs spread widely across Europe.

In the Hallingdalo region of Norway, wrist warmers were a common part of the men's national costume. They were described as "ornamental accessories," and they are still worn today, and not only with the national costume[5].

In the Lovice region of Poland, wrist warmers are an important part of the men's national costume[6].

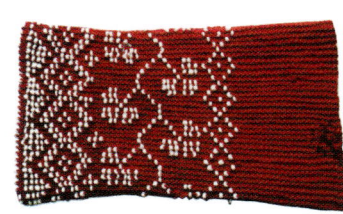

6

Around 1980, the Czech physicist Svetla Vackova saw my wrist warmers and said: "My grandmother always wore these, with any clothes." In the south of France, women's national costumes included knitted or crocheted cotton mitts with half fingers (French "*mitaines*") . While I was collecting material for this book, I asked whether these were made of wool for winter. It turned out that they were not wool, but they were made with longer cuffs for the colder weather. In Estonia, wrist warmers were worn by islanders and coastal residents. These wrist warmers were knitted with the same techniques used to knit the cuffs on gloves. In the late nineteenth century, they were worn by

7

10a

10

---

[7] Photo by Loïc Salfati.
[8] Kalju Konsin. *Silmkoeesemed. Eesti rahvakunst I*. Tallinn: "Kunst" 1972. Information received from Igoris Tonurist.
[9] Information provided by Ulia Gintnerė, Liepāja Museum.
[10], [10a] Information provided by Astra Dzervė, Liepāja Museum.
[11] Information provided by Sviatlana Klepikava (Minsk, Belarus).
[12] Ibid.

11 12

both men and women[8].

Latvians have not only preserved examples of old wrist warmers in museums, but the tradition is gradually being revived as a contemporary fashion[9, 10].

In Belarus (east of Lithuania), there are no wrist warmers in museum collections, but today they are very popular, especially with young people [11, 12].

According to ethnographers, most of the wrist warmers in Lithuania's museums were made in the late nineteenth and the early twentieth century. Later, when wrist warmers fell out of fashion, many women unraveled theirs, and used the yarn to make gloves, mittens, collars, and other accessories.

While most of the surviving examples of wrist warmers in museum collections today are from Žemaitija (northwestern Lithuania), examples from throughout Lithuania are not uncommon.

Lithuanian Wrist Warmer Styles

In Lithuania, knitted wrist warmers were anywhere from 2–7½ inches (4.5–19 cm) long. Everyday wrist warmers were made out of whatever wool yarn was available, often handspun. Sometimes old, faded garments were unraveled and the yarn was re-used. These casual accessories were knitted with thick needles out of heavy woolen yarn. Some were also crocheted. They were made to fit snugly, and were knit in a single color, either lengthwise or sideways. There are also examples of wrist warmers made in a "hit-or-miss" pattern, where it seems like the knitter used all of her leftover scraps of yarn, changing colors randomly.

Holiday wrist warmers were made using high-quality, fine wool yarn—usually a special commercially-spun yarn called *lučkai*. Some were made in stockinette stitch with stranded colorwork patterns, and knit in the round. The most decorative wrist warmers were knit back and forth, sideways, in garter stitch (knit on both right-side and wrong-side rows) creating a stretchy rib pattern. White beads, or less frequently colored beads, were knit in to create the pattern. These wrist warmers were worn because of their beauty, not for practical reasons.

There are two unusual pairs of wrist warmers with the bead patterns worked in embroidery. One example from Druskininkai is in The Open-Air Museum of Lithuania. The wrist warmer is

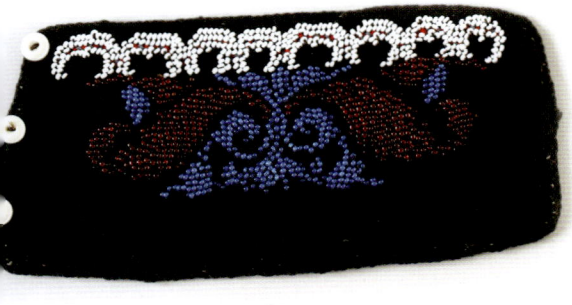

made in knit one, purl one ribbing, and white beads are sewn on in a decorative pattern (figure 15 on page 155). Another example in the collections of the M. K. Čiurlionis National Museum of Art is from the village of Rinkuškiai in Birzai District. This wrist warmer is knit in black with a fir tree or herringbone pattern embroidered with white beads along the edge, and a stylized leaf motif in the center made with red and blue beads. This wrist warmer is knit flat and closes with small buttons.

The motifs used on wrist warmers are similar throughout Lithuania. These include eight-pointed stars, fir trees, zigzags, flowers, diamonds, crosses, and triangles.

In Aukštaitija (northeastern Lithuania), wrist warmers were most commonly found in the northern part of Birzai, and a few examples are from the areas of Kedainiai, Kupiškis, Pasvalys, Rokiškis, Šiauliai, Ukmerge, and Zarasai. The patterns on wrist warmers in Aukštaitija were most often knit in bold colors, such as black, brown, red, cherry, green, or blue, and embellished with white beads. In Birzai, women also knitted wrist warmers using yarn scraps to make three-colored stripes, with a bead pattern of white roses ("Lists of Exhibits of the Folk Art Department of the Biržai Museum," Archival Book, Record No. 1034 of 19 May 1932). In addition, there are single-color wrist warmers decorated with several colors of beads.

Wrist warmers made in the northwest (Šiauliai County, Šiaulėnai State, Liepiškiai District) are sometimes knit in four color stripes of black, green, red and blue, and are decorated with white beads.

The wrist warmers made in Dzūkija (southeastern Lithuania) are very colorful, knit in black, burgundy, rust, blue, dark blue, and purple, and they are also very decorative. Most museum samples from this region have been gathered from the Lazdijai and Prienai districts. Other examples are from the districts of Alytus, Trakai, and Seina (now in Poland). Patterns of white, yellow, and red beads were

common. The wrist edge of the piece was also often decorated with beaded trim.

In the Suvalkija region (southwestern Lithuania), all women wore wrist warmers in the winter. The most popular color for yarn was blue-violet, and beads were typically white. The patterns are similar to those in other ethnographic regions.

In Žemaitija (northwestern Lithuania), wrist warmers were also very widespread. They were found in the districts of Akmenė, Kelmė, Kretinga, Mažeikiai, Plungė, Raseiniai, Skuodas, Šilalė, Tauragė, and Telšiai. The background was usually knitted in stripes of two contrasting colors, such as red and blue, purple and green, or black and green, but there were also three- and four-colored wrist warmers decorated with patterns of white beads. Solid wrist warmers in Žemaitija were made dark colors, including black, brass, dark brown, and purple. They were decorated not only with white beads, but also with colored beads.

Wrist warmers were also made in the region of Klaipėda. From the surviving examples it is possible to judge that the most popular patterns were diamond lattices, made in various colors for everyday wear. There are no holiday wrist warmers from this region surviving in museum collections. I knitted the sample in this book using black wool with white beads, following an illustration I found in the book *Gloves of Lithuania Minor*. (*Lietuvininkų pirštinės* Lithuanian Ethnology, 3, by Irena Regina Merkienė, Marija Pautieniute-Banionienė. Vilnius: Žara. 1998, pg. 191).

Mitts and fingerless gloves in Lithuania were sometimes knitted and crocheted from linen and cotton thread (figure 50, page 171). Appendix 2 contains examples of fingerless gloves and cotton mitts[13] with thumbs that vary from ½–1 inch (1.5–2 cm) long, as well as one example with half-fingers. Most of these are from Žemaitija; one is from the Klaipeda region. These gloves were knitted or crochet in lace patterns to be worn on special occasions by brides (figures 6 and 174) and flower-girls (figure 1, 172, p. 5, 173). Other gloves, made in stockinette stitch, were made to wear as gardening gloves in summer, to protect the wearer's hands while working outdoors.

[13] The words in Eastern Lithuanian dialects are *pirštinės pirštas* (gloves with fingers), *su pirštikais pirštinės šaltos* (gloves with cold fingers) in Švenčionys, and *pirštinės trumpas pirštikas* (gloves with short fingers), and *kumštinės pirštinės nykštys* (mitts with thumbs) in Rokiškis. *Lietuvių kalbos žodynas*, Volume 10, Vilnius, 1976, page 32.

Knitting Beaded Wrist Warmers

Here are the basic instructions for knitting Lithuanian beaded wrist warmers.

Materials

About 150 yards (140 m) of fingering-weight or heavy lace-weight wool yarn
Glass seed beads (the number of beads for each pattern is listed with the charts)
US size 0000 or 000 (1.25 or 1.5 mm) needles, or size to get a firm gauge that will hold the beads in place.
Beading needle
Tapestry needle or crochet hook for seaming

You can find glass seed beads of various sizes at bead stores, craft stores, and online. When buying beads, it's important to be sure they have holes large enough to fit the yarn through. If you have trouble threading your yarn on the needle, you can use a needle threader tool for assistance (figure 1, page 20).

The most suitable glass beads are size 8/0 or size 10/0 seed beads. Smaller beads, such as size 11/0, are also used on the samples in the Lithuanian museums—but they can be nearly impossible to string onto fingering weight yarn.

A Short History of Glass Seed Beads

Encyclopedias and various other sources state that glass is one of the most important materials used in the production of beads. In Egypt and the Middle East, glass beads have been used for at least 2000 years. They were most often used to make jewelry.

In the Roman era, Alexandria was the world's largest supplier of glass beads. During the Byzantine era (Eastern Roman Empire), the art of making glassware arrived in Italy, and from there the production of glass beads spread throughout Europe. Today, the main suppliers of glass beads to Lithuania are the Czech Republic, Germany, Slovakia, and India. In the United States, Czech and Japanese seed beads are most popular and easiest to find in stores.

Glass beads were introduced to Lithuania from other countries. By the ninth to thirteenth centuries, Lithuania already had established trade relations with the West, Eastern Europe, and Middle Eastern countries. It is believed that beads came to Lithuania from the Byzantine Empire and other Middle Eastern countries[14].

Small seed beads were used to make necklaces, as well as to decorate head coverings and boxes made from beech bark. Because beads were so expensive and highly valued at that time, a beaded necklace was not only a beautiful piece of jewelry, but also a sign of wealth.

Since the late nineteenth century, colored glass seed beads have been widely used in Lithuania for handcrafts: they were first used to embellish clothes, embroidered pictures, tablecloths, and collars. More recently, seed beads have also been used for knitting jabots, wrist warmers, and change purses [15].

Beading. ČDM E 4698

[14] O. Kuncienė. *IX-XIII a. stiklo karoliai Lietuvoje.* // Lietuvos archeologija No. 2, 1981, pages 77-90.
[15] L. Gaigalienė. *XVI – XIX a. Siuviniai. Katalogas* // LTSR Istorijos ir etnogra jos muziejaus leidinys. Vilnius, 1988, pages 5-6.

Beaded wallet from Aukštaitijos. ČDM E 6610

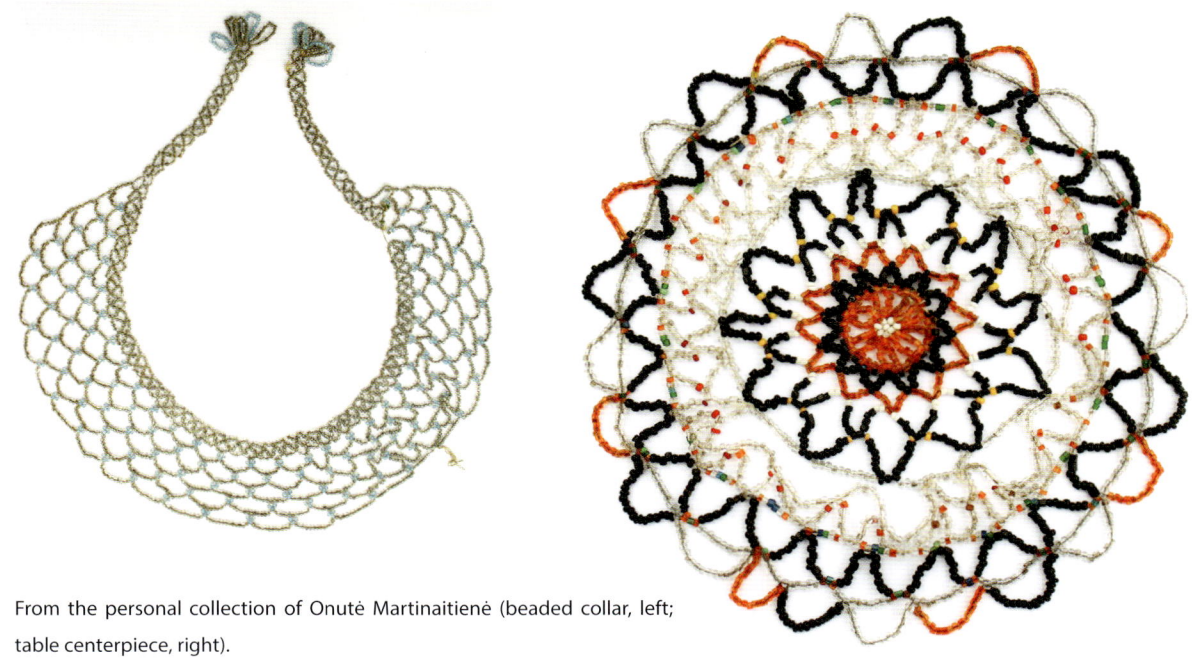

From the personal collection of Onutė Martinaitienė (beaded collar, left; table centerpiece, right).

Instructions

Before starting, you need to know how many beads are needed for one wrist warmer. Two to three hundred might be enough for a simple pattern, whereas a complicated pattern can sometimes take up to 1200 or 1500 beads. (The number of beads needed for each chart is listed on the page with the chart. Always string on extra beads in case you miscount. Seed beads are sold by weight, so you will have to check the number of beads per gram for the beads you select.)

Tip: To make the process quicker, count the first hundred beads, and then measure the remaining beads you thread on against this (figure 4) to estimate additional hundreds. If using more than one color of beads, string them on following the chart.

Thread the yarn onto a very thin beading needle. If the holes in the beads are large enough, you can easily slide the beads onto the yarn with a large-eyed beading needle. If the holes or needle-eye are too small, you can use a piece of strong sewing thread as a leader. To do this, glue the tail end of the thread to the tail end of the yarn using adhesive for repairing shoes (I use Pattex Contact for Shoes and Leather). Let it dry completely, then thread the needle with the sewing thread.

Pour the beads into a small, shallow bowl or a dish especially designed for this purpose. Move the needle back and forth in the beads as shown in figure 2. In this way, several beads can be loaded onto the needle at once. Then slide the beads onto the yarn. If you are using sewing thread as a leader, carefully slide the beads up the thread, past the join, and onto the yarn (figure 3).

Slide groups of beads further up onto the yarn so they are evenly distributed (figure 5) and out of the way for knitting. You will need about 77 yards (70 m) of very fine wool yarn for each wrist warmer[16].

For a wrist warmer 4 inches (10 cm) long, cast on about 50 stitches. (The exact length will depend on your gauge.) Work back and forth in garter stitch (knit on right-side and wrong-side rows), and as you knit, pull a few beads down closer to your needles at the beginning of each chart row. The beads are knit in on the wrong-side rows following the chart (figure 6). After each beaded row, work a plain row without beads. Each row of the chart represents a

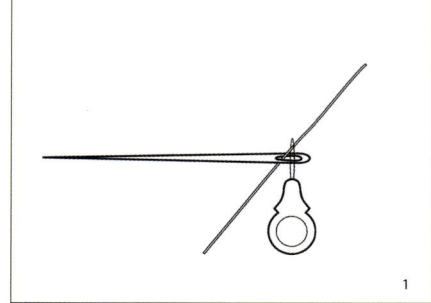

1

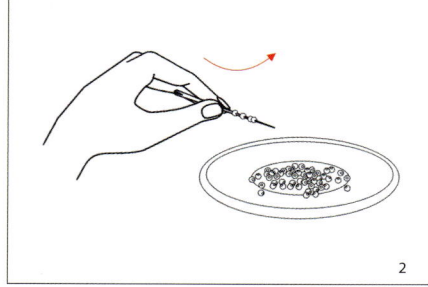

2

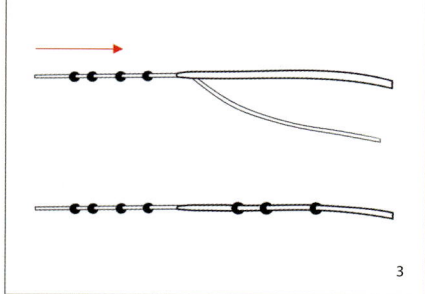

3

---

[16] The author uses Latvian wool yarn and Czech seed beads.

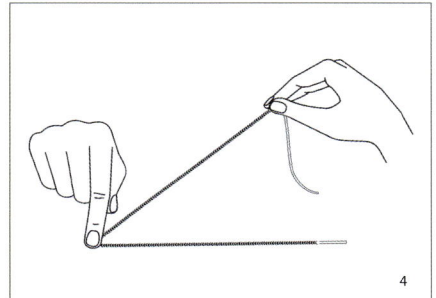

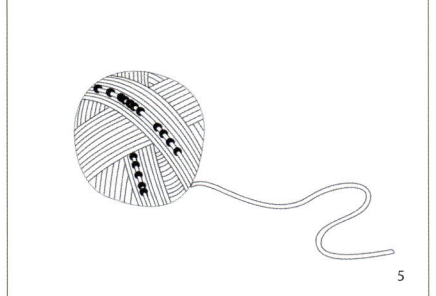

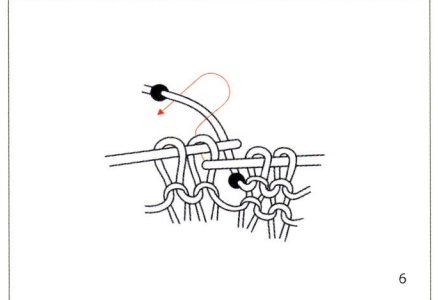

wrong-side (beaded) row and the right-side plain row that follows it. Work the number of rows specified for each chart, or until the piece is wide enough to reach around your wrist. Then bind off and seam the CO and BO edges together.

Wrist warmers can be finished with a crochet trim worked on the right side of the work. The trim can be made with crochet chain picots or double-crochet shells worked in a circle around the wrist edge. Adding a beaded picot trim at the wrist edge will make the wrist warmers even more decorative.

Beading Charts and Knitted Samples

1.

Wrist warmers
Made in the area of Biržai, Lithuania
BKM GEK 825[17]

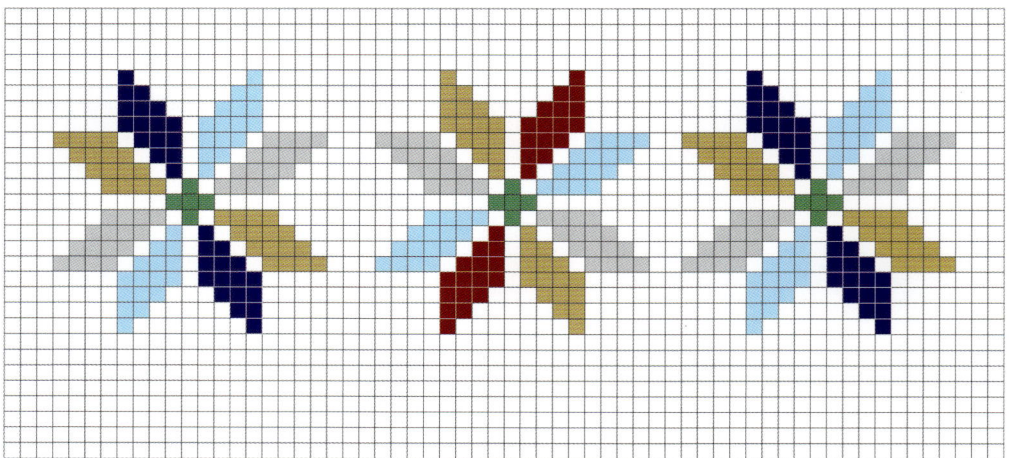

Skill Level: Intermediate
Beads: 256 each of light blue, gray, and beige; 128 each of dark blue and red, 32 green
String beads onto yarn following chart. Cast on 40–50 sts for desired length.
Knit all RS rows. On WS rows, work all sts of the bead chart, then knit to the end of the row. Work all rows or chart once, then work one more repeat of the center flower/star and end with 2 plain rows. BO, then sew CO and BO edges together.
With contrasting yarn, work 1 row of single crochet around one edge of wrist warmer.
Make a second wrist warmer the same way.

---

[17] For each pattern, the original wrist warmers are shown on the right-hand page, with the knitting chart and details on the left.

| **2.** | AUKŠTAITIJA (NORTHEASTERN LITHUANIA)

| 3. |

Wrist warmers
Made in the village of Deikiškiai,
Vabalninkas County, in the region of
Biržai, Lithuania
BKM GEK 3557

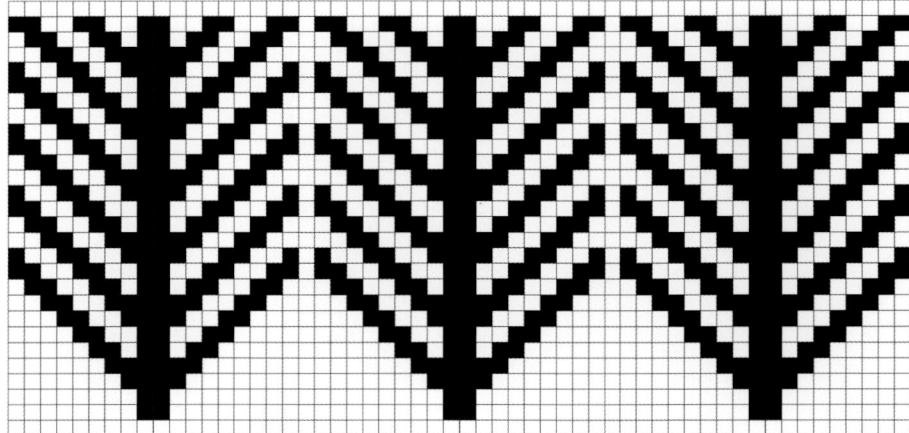

Skill Level: Intermediate
Beads: 896 white (224 per pattern repeat)
String half of beads onto yarn. Cast on 40–50 sts for desired length.

Knit all RS rows. On WS rows, work all sts of the bead chart, then knit to the end of the row. Work all rows of chart, then work one more motif and end with 2 plain rows. BO, then sew CO and BO edges together. Make a second wrist warmer the same way.

| **4.** | Aukštaitija (Northeastern Lithuania)

5.

Men's wrist warmers / *rankovėlės*
Late 19th century
Made in Pabiržė District, Biržai County, Lithuania
ČDM E 1547/a, b

Skill Level: Intermediate
Beads: 1490 white
Other Materials: Yarn in contrasting color and crochet hook for edging
String half of beads onto yarn. Cast on 40–50 sts for desired length.

Knit all RS rows. On WS rows, work all sts of the bead chart, then knit to the end of the row. Work all rows of chart once. BO, then sew CO and BO edges together. With contrasting yarn, work 1 row of single crochet around one edge of wrist warmer.
Make a second wrist warmer the same way.

| 6. | AUKŠTAITIJA (NORTHEASTERN LITHUANIA)

7.

Wrist warmers / *rankovėlės*
19th century
Made in the village of Užugulbinė,
Pabiržė District, Biržai County, Lithuania
ČDM E 1549/a, b

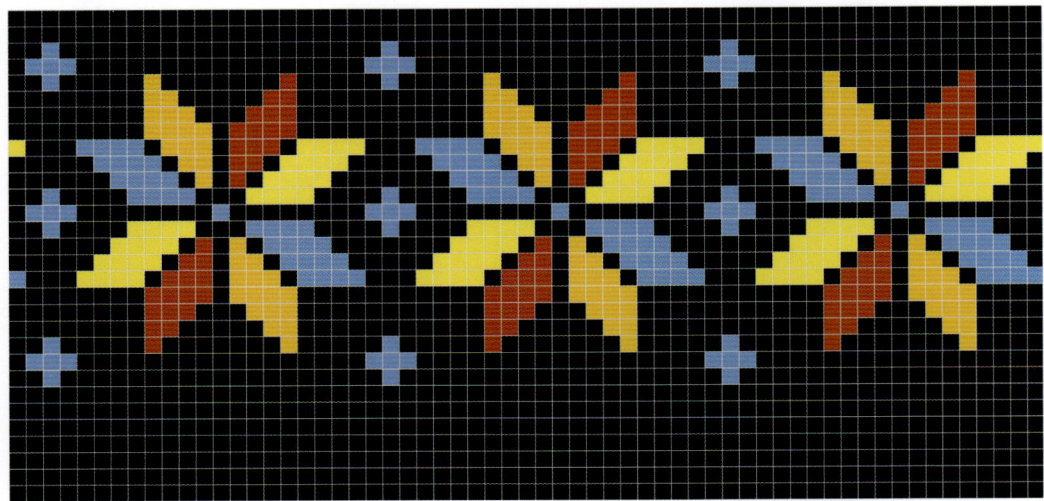

Skill Level: Intermediate
Beads: 256 each of red, yellow, and gold; 328 blue
String beads onto yarn following chart. Cast on 40–50 sts for desired length.
Knit all RS rows. On WS rows, work all sts of the bead chart, then knit to the end of the row. Work to last row of chart, then work one more flower/star motif and with the last row of the chart to match the pattern to the beginning. BO, then sew CO and BO edges together.
Make a second wrist warmer the same way.

| 8. | AUKŠTAITIJA (NORTHEASTERN LITHUANIA)

 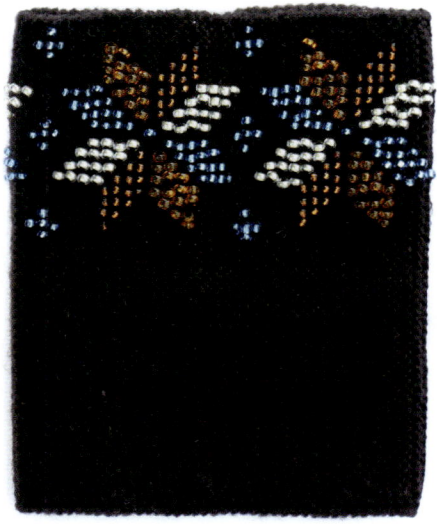

9.

Glove
Made in the village of Užugulbinė,
Pabiržės District, Biržai County, Lithuania
ČDM E 1573

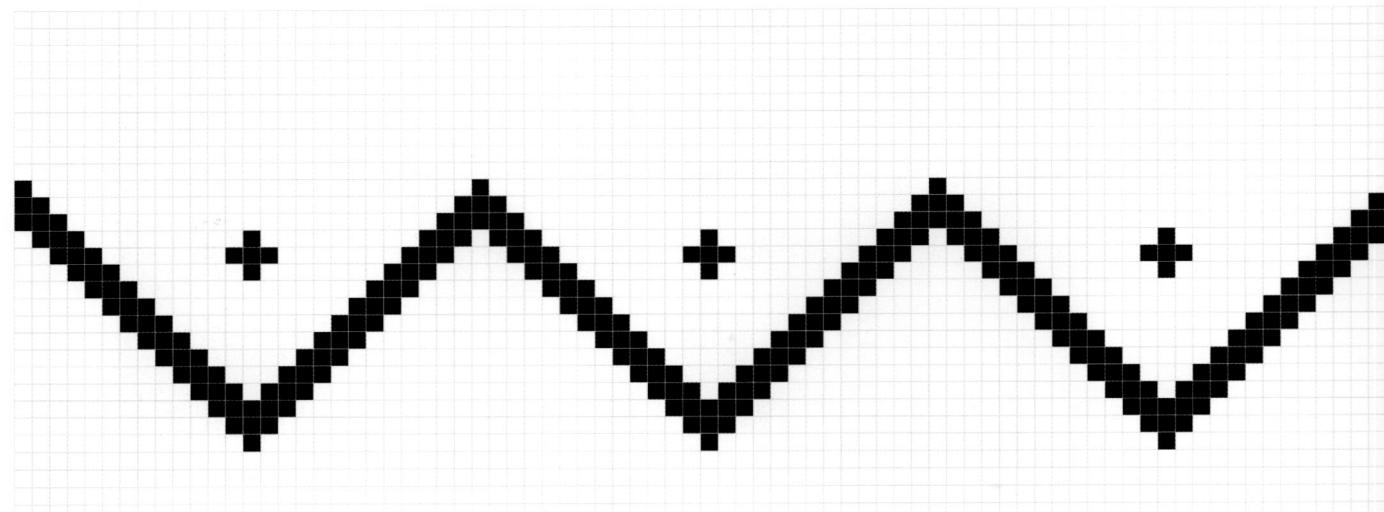

Skill Level: Intermediate
Beads: 534 white
String half of beads onto yarn. Cast on 40–50 sts for desired length.

Knit all RS rows. On WS rows, work all sts of the bead chart, then knit to the end of the row. Work all rows of chart once. BO, then sew CO and BO edges together. Make a second wrist warmer the same way.

| **10.** | Aukštaitija (Northeastern Lithuania)

11.

Wrist warmers / *rankovėlės*
19th century
Made in the village of Rinkuškiai,
Biržai District, Biržai County, Lithuania
ČDM E 1575/a, b

Skill Level: Intermediate
Beads: 1490 white for main pattern + 55 for monogram
String half of beads onto yarn. Cast on 40–50 sts for desired length.

Knit all RS rows. On WS rows, work all sts of the bead chart, then knit to the end of the row. Work all rows of chart, omitting monogram if desired. BO, then sew CO and BO edges together.
Make a second wrist warmer the same way.

| **12.** | AUKŠTAITIJA (NORTHEASTERN LITHUANIA)

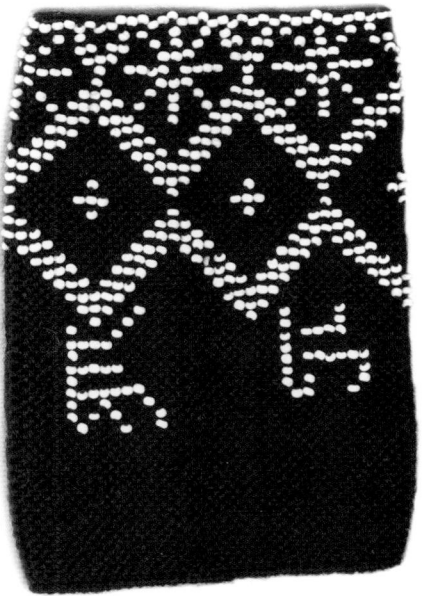

13.

Embellished wrist warmers / *rankovėlės*
Early 20th century
Knit by O. D. Aleknienė.
Made in the village of Rinkuškiai, Biržai District,
Biržai County, Lithuania
ČDM E 1550/a, b

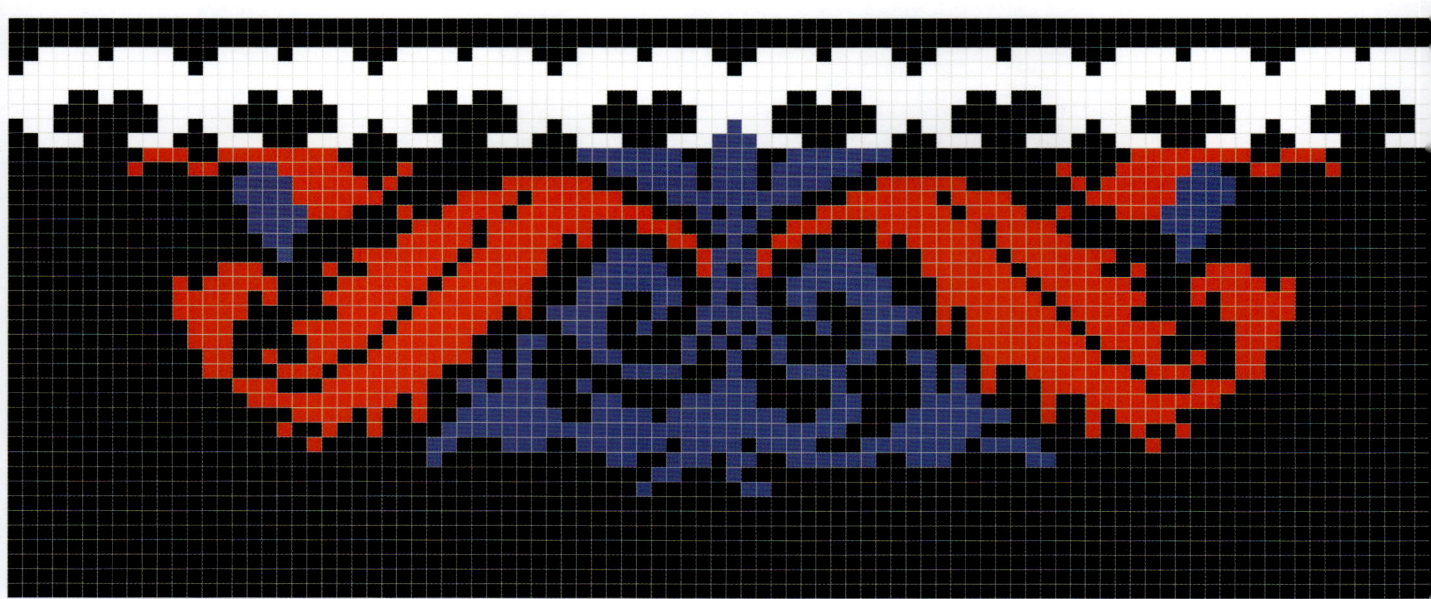

Skill Level: Intermediate
Beads: 800 white, 312 red, and 380 blue
String beads onto yarn following chart. Cast on 40–50 sts for desired length.

Knit all RS rows. On WS rows, work all sts of the bead chart, then knit to the end of the row. Work all rows of chart once. BO, then sew CO and BO edges together. Make a second wrist warmer the same way.

| **14.** | Aukštaitija (Northeastern Lithuania)

| **15.** |

Men's wrist warmers / *runkauka*
Late 19th century
Made at the farmstead of Kvietkeliai,
Biržai County, Lithuania
LNM EMO1601

16. AUKŠTAITIJA (NORTHEASTERN LITHUANIA)

Skill Level: Intermediate
Beads: 2844 white, 504 blue, and 42 red
String beads onto yarn following chart. Cast on 40–50 sts for desired length.
Knit all RS rows. On WS rows, work all sts of the bead chart, then knit to the end of the row. Work a I rows of chart once, then work one more repeat of pattern (one star and one flower motif). BO, then sew CO and BO edges together.
Make a second wrist warmer the same way.

17.

Wrist warmers / *rankovėlės*
Made in Biržai County, Lithuania
ČDM E 1546/a, b

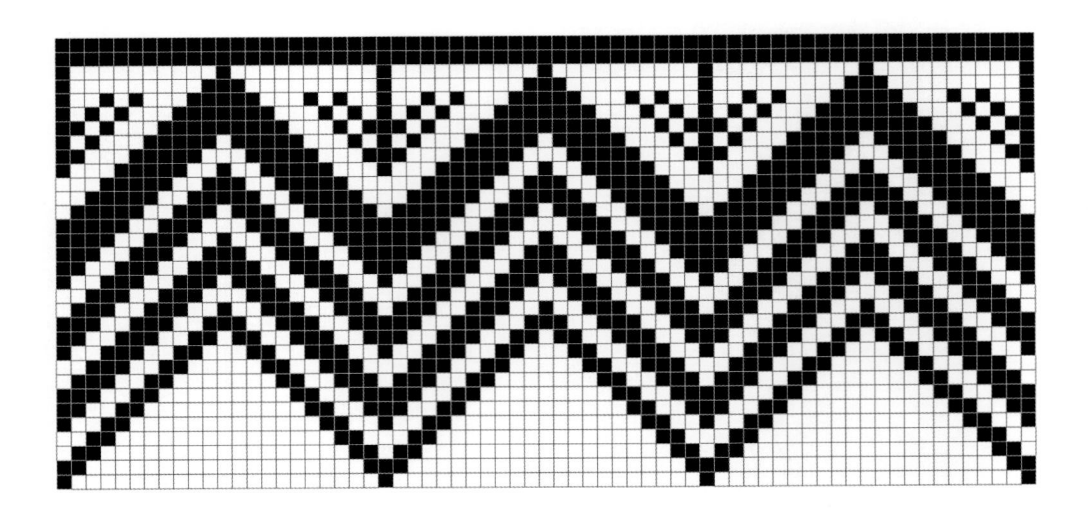

Skill Level: Intermediate
Beads: 2136 white
String half of beads onto yarn. Cast on 40–50 sts for desired length.

Knit all RS rows. On WS rows, work all sts of the bead chart, then knit to the end of the row. Work all rows of chart once. BO, then sew CO and BO edges together. Make a second wrist warmer the same way.

| **18.** | AUKŠTAITIJA (NORTHEASTERN LITHUANIA)

| **19.** |

Wrist warmers / *rankovėlės*
Made in the village of Pilsupiai,
Josvainiai District, Kėdainiai, Lithuania
ČDM E 1567/a, b

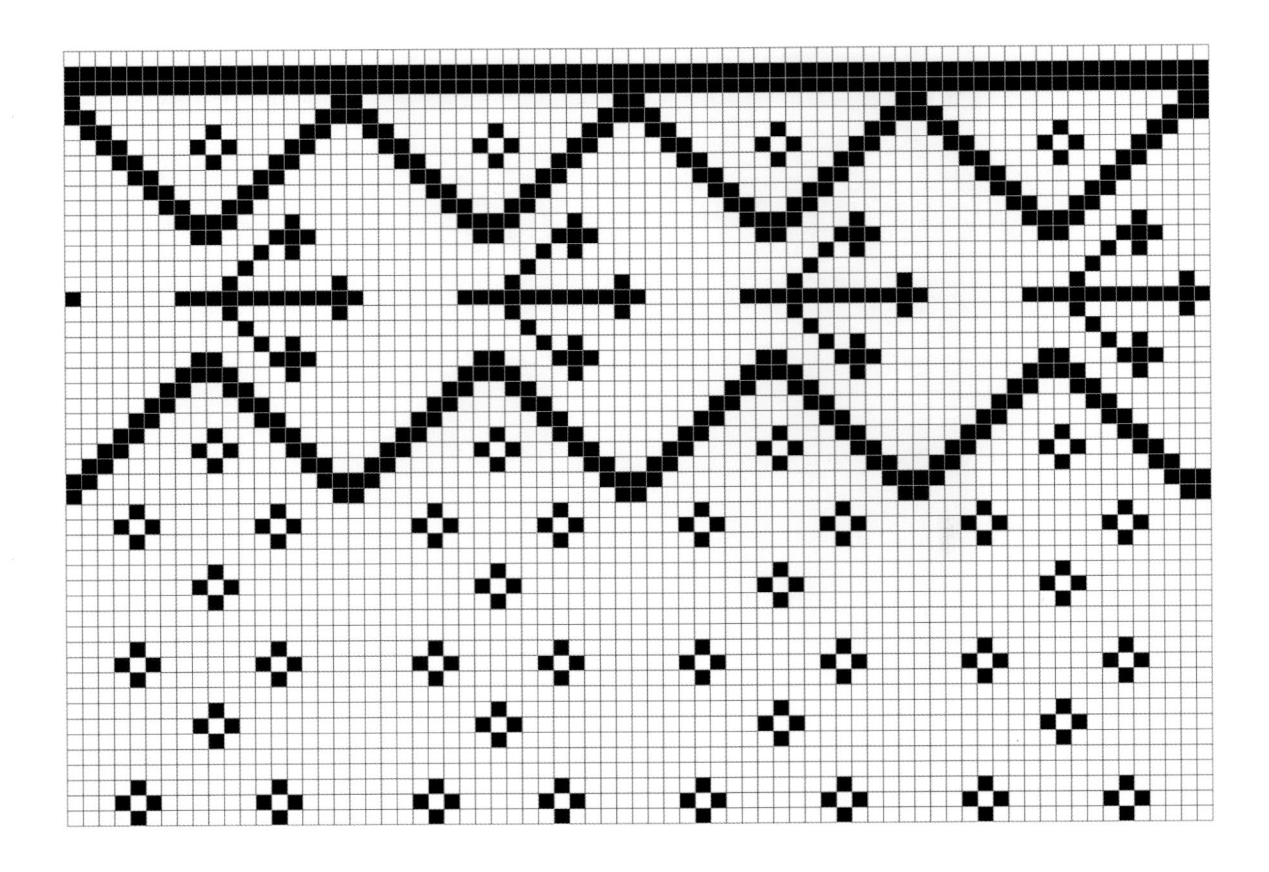

20.   AUKŠTAITIJA (NORTHEASTERN LITHUANIA)

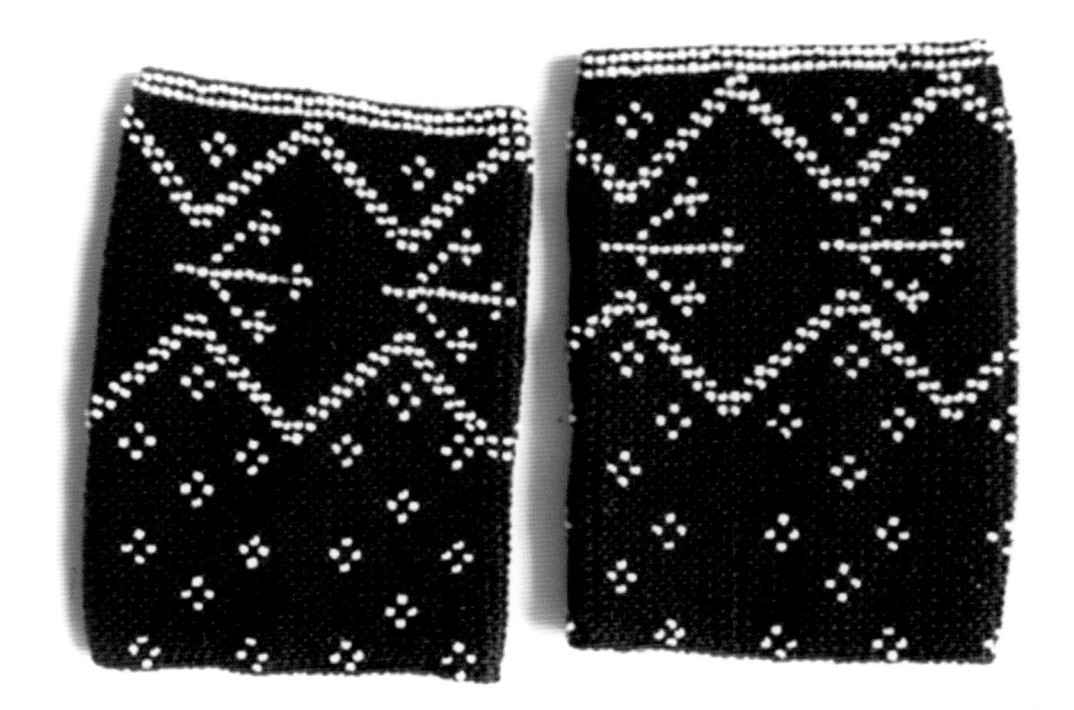

Skill Level: Intermediate
Beads: 1424 white
String half of beads onto yarn. Cast on 40–50 sts for desired length.

Knit all RS rows. On WS rows, work all sts of the bead chart, then knit to the end of the row. Work all rows of chart once. BO, then sew CO and BO edges together. Make a second wrist warmer the same way.

21.

Dicky
Late 19th century
Made in Pasvalis County, Lithuania
Bead pattern adapted for wrist warmers
ČDM E 3869

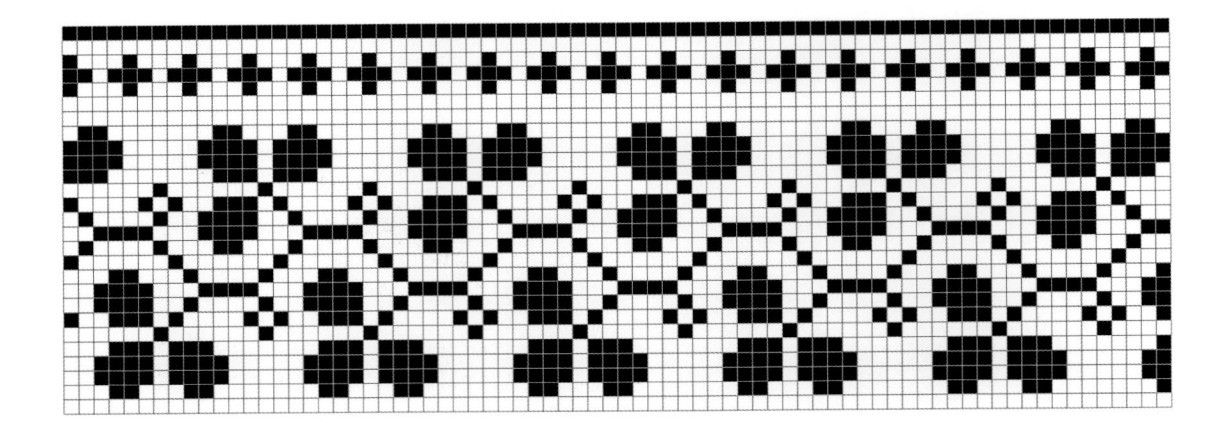

Skill Level: Intermediate
Beads: 1380 white
String half of beads onto yarn. Cast on 40–50 sts for desired length.

Knit all RS rows. On WS rows, work all sts of the bead chart, then knit to the end of the row. Work all rows of chart once. BO, then sew CO and BO edges together. Make a second wrist warmer the same way.

| **22.** | Aukštaitija (Northeastern Lithuania)

23.

Wrist warmers
Early 20th century
Made in Linkuva, in the region of Pakruojis, Lithuania
From Živilė Jurevičiūtė-Ramelienė's personal collection.

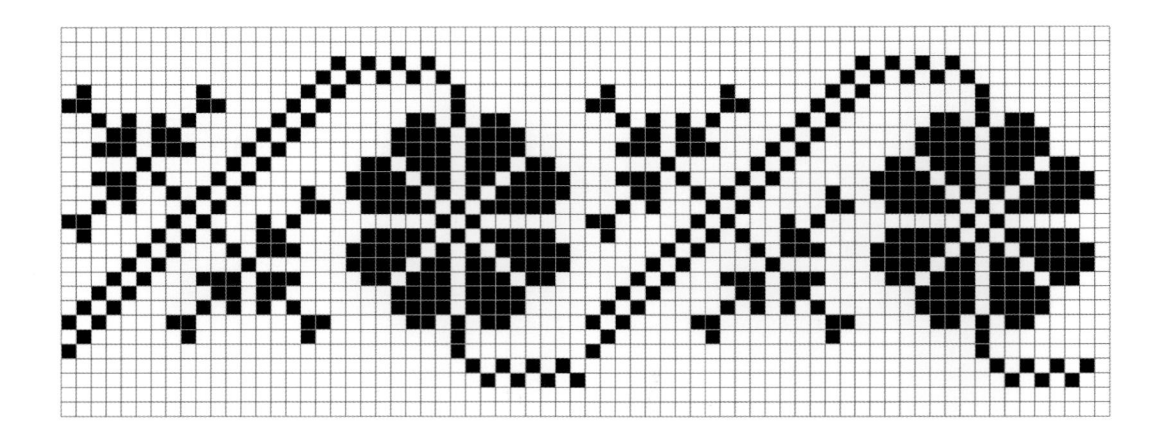

Skill Level: Intermediate
Beads: 1024 white
String half of beads onto yarn. Cast on 40–50 sts for desired length.

Knit all RS rows. On WS rows, work all sts of the bead chart, then knit to the end of the row. Work all rows of chart once. BO, then sew CO and BO edges together. Make a second wrist warmer the same way.

| **24.** | AUKŠTAITIJA (NORTHEASTERN LITHUANIA)

25.

Wrist warmers / *rankaukos*
19th century
From the village of Liūneliai, Vidiškiai County, in the region of Ukmergė, Lithuania
LDM LA 2318/a,b

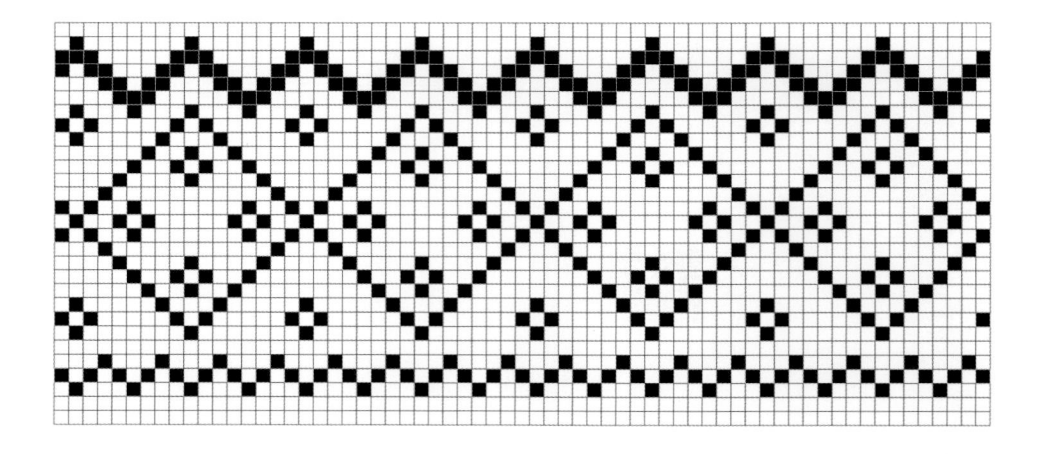

Skill Level: Intermediate
Beads: 832 white
String half of beads onto yarn. Cast on 40–50 sts for desired length.

Knit all RS rows. On WS rows, work all sts of the bead chart, then knit to the end of the row. Work all rows of chart once. BO, then sew CO and BO edges together. Make a second wrist warmer the same way.

| **26.** | Aukštaitija (Northeastern Lithuania)

27.

Wrist warmers / *rankauka*
Early 20th century
Made in the village of Rudikuai, Kupiškis District, Panevėžys County, Lithuania
ŠAM EO 467

Skill Level: Intermediate
Beads: 1008 white
String half of beads onto yarn. Cast on 40–50 sts for desired length.

Knit all RS rows. On WS rows, work all sts of the bead chart, then knit to the end of the row. Work all rows of chart once. BO, then sew CO and BO edges together. Make a second wrist warmer the same way.

| **28.** | AUKŠTAITIJA (NORTHEASTERN LITHUANIA)

29.

Wrist warmers
19th century
Made in the village of Varniškis,
Antašava County, in the region of
Kupiškis, Lithuania
LDM LA 1466/a,b

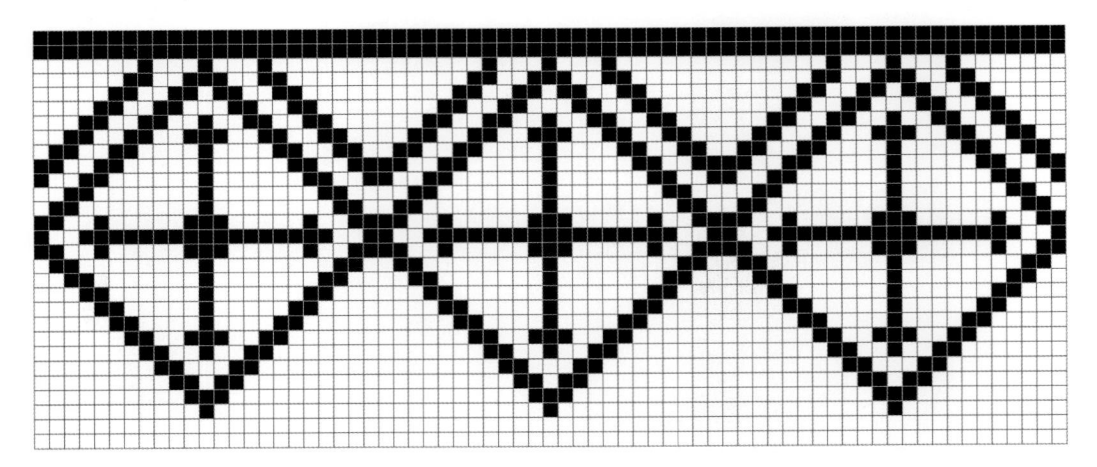

Skill Level: Intermediate
Beads: 1374 white
String half of beads onto yarn. Cast on 40–50 sts for desired length.

Knit all RS rows. On WS rows, work all sts of the bead chart, then knit to the end of the row. Work all rows of chart once. BO, then sew CO and BO edges together. Make a second wrist warmer the same way.

| **30.** | AUKŠTAITIJA (NORTHEASTERN LITHUANIA)

31.

Wrist warmers / *rukavicos*
Late 19th century
Made in the village of Laibgaliai, Rokiškis District, Rokiškis County, Lithuania
LNM EMO 6339/a,b

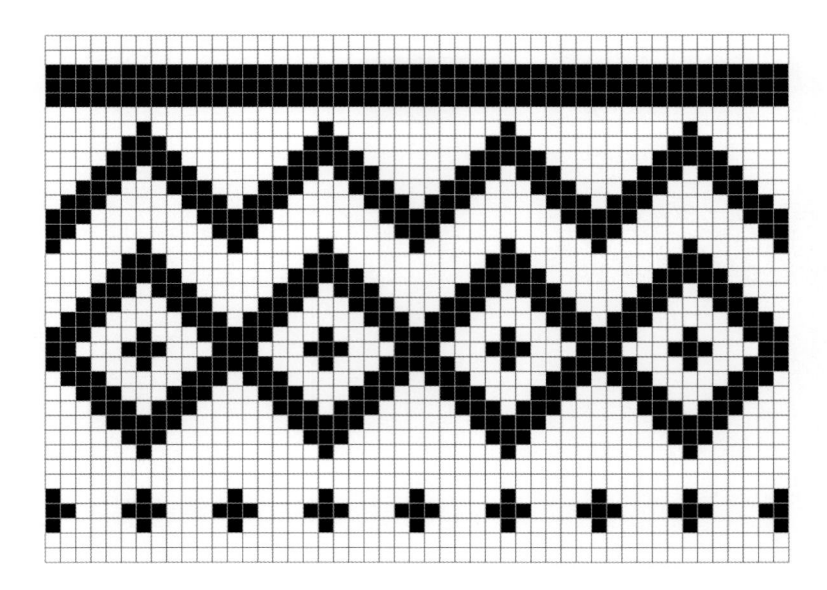

Skill Level: Intermediate
Beads: 1824 white
String half of beads onto yarn. Cast on 40–50 sts for desired length.

Knit all RS rows. On WS rows, work all sts of the bead chart, then knit to the end of the row. Work all rows of chart, then work 2 more diamond repeats. BO, then sew CO and BO edges together.
Make a second wrist warmer the same way.

| **32.** | Aukštaitija (Northeastern Lithuania)

33.

Wrist warmer / *rankovėlė*
Late 19th century
Made in the village of Liepiškiai, Šiauliai District, Šiaulėnai County, Lithuania
ČDM E 1566

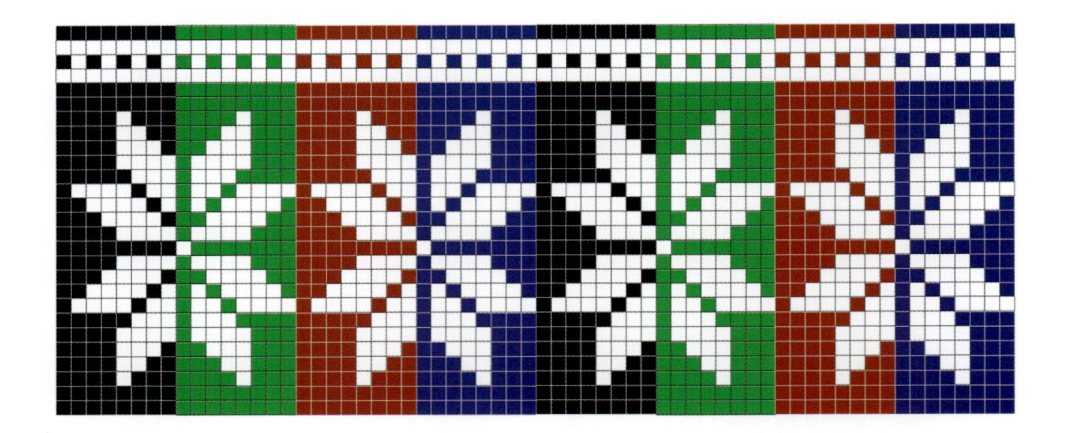

Skill Level: Experienced
Beads: 1352 white
Yarn Colors: blue, red, green, and black
String one-quarter of beads onto each color of yarn. Cast on 40–50 sts for desired length.

Knit all RS rows. On WS rows, work all sts of the bead chart, then knit to the end of the row. Work all rows of chart, changing colors on WS (beaded) rows. BO, then sew CO and BO edges together.
Make a second wrist warmer the same way.

| **34.** | Aukštaitija (Northeastern Lithuania)

| **35.** |

Wrist warmer
Made in Rumšiškis County, in the
region of Kaunas, Lithuania
LNM EMO 1856

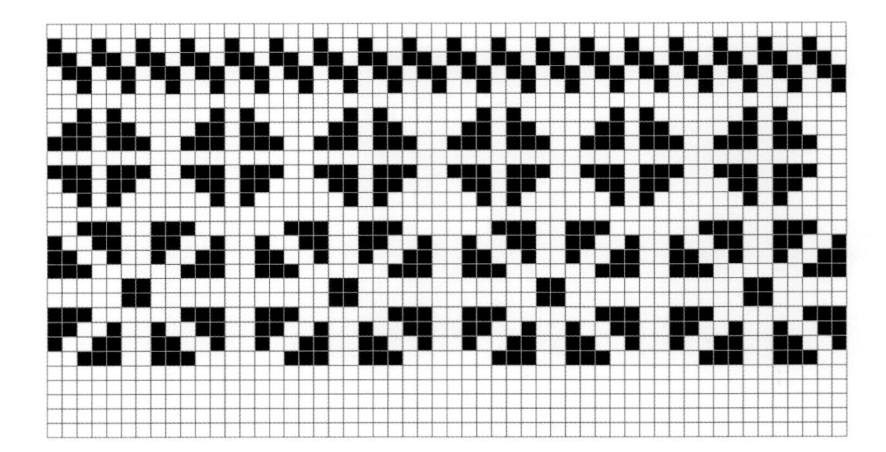

Skill Level: Intermediate
Beads: 1420 white
String half of beads onto yarn. Cast on 40–50 sts for desired length.
Knit all RS rows. On WS rows, work all sts of the bead chart, then knit to the end of the row. Work all rows of chart once, then work one more pattern repeat of flower, matching up alignment of smaller patterns. BO, then sew CO and BO edges together.
Make a second wrist warmer the same way.

| **36.** | AUKŠTAITIJA (NORTHEASTERN LITHUANIA)

37.

Wrist warmers
Late 19th century
Made in the village of Geruliai, Balbieriškis
County, in the region of Prienai, Lithuania
LDM LA 1946/a,b

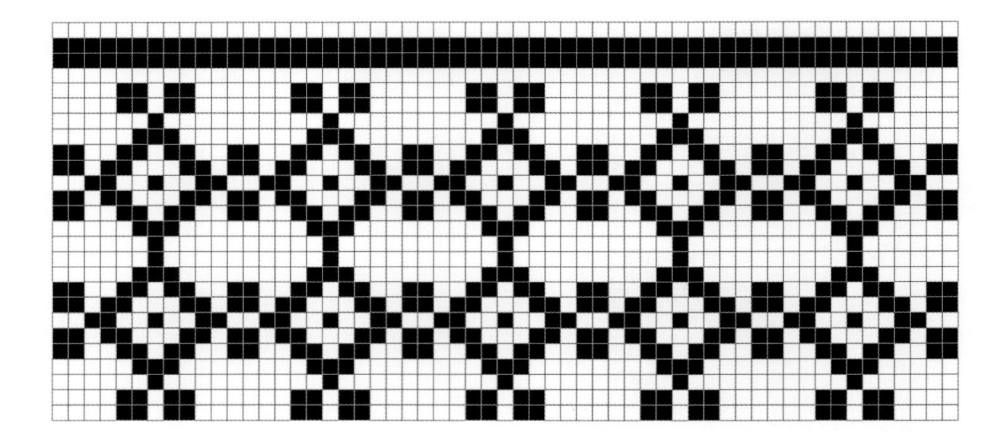

Skill Level: Intermediate
Beads: 1104 white
String half of beads onto yarn. Cast on 40–50 sts for desired length.
Knit all RS rows. On WS rows, work all sts of the bead chart, then knit to the end of the row. Work all rows of chart once, then work one more repeat of diamonds, ending after before the squares to match beginning of piece. BO, then sew CO and BO edges together. Make a second wrist warmer the same way.

| **38.** | Dzūkija (Southeastern Lithuania)

39.

Wrist warmers / *rankapkos*
Late 19th century
Made in the village of Norkūnai, Balbieriškis County, in the region of Prienai, Lithuania
LNM EMO 3892/a,b

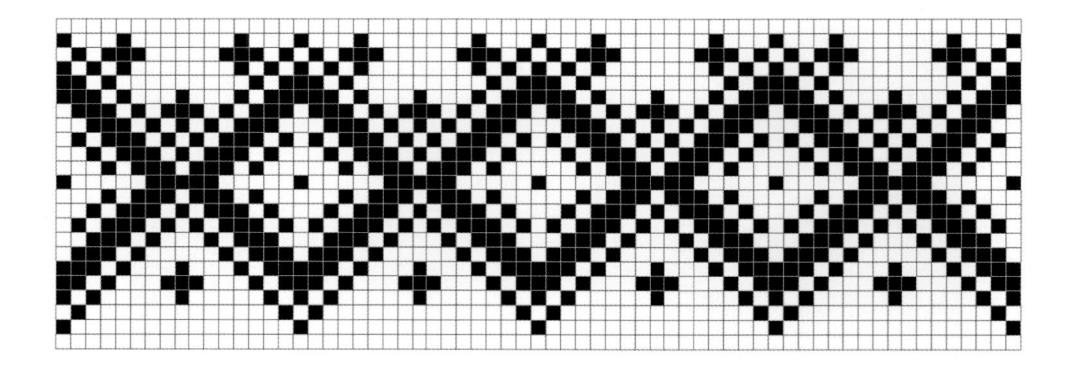

Skill Level: Intermediate
Beads: 1144 white
String half of beads onto yarn. Cast on 40–50 sts for desired length.

Knit all RS rows. On WS rows, work all sts of the bead chart, then knit to the end of the row. Work all rows of chart once. BO, then sew CO and BO edges together. Make a second wrist warmer the same way.

| **40.** | Dzūkija (Southeastern Lithuania)

41.

Wrist warmers / *rankapkos*
Late 19th century
Made in the village of Norkūnai, Balbieriškis
County, in the region of Prienai, Lithuania
LNM EMO 3891/a,b

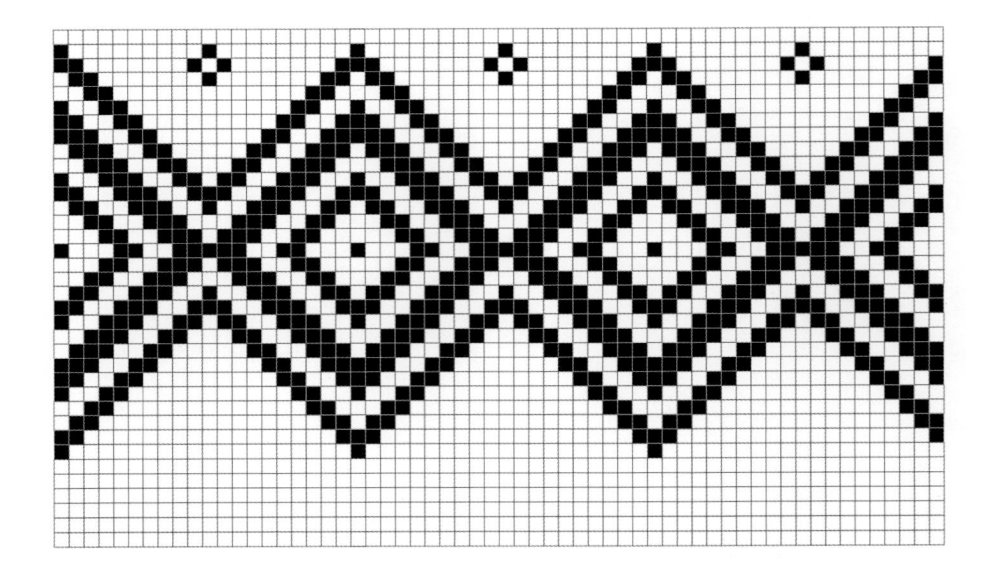

Skill Level: Intermediate
Beads: 750 white
String half of beads onto yarn. Cast on 40–50 sts for desired length.

Knit all RS rows. On WS rows, work all sts of the bead chart, then knit to the end of the row. Work all rows of chart once. BO, then sew CO and BO edges together. Make a second wrist warmer the same way.

| **42.** | DZŪKIJA (SOUTHEASTERN LITHUANIA)

43.

Wrist warmers / *rankovėlės*
Early 20th century
Made in the village of Naudžiūnuai, Birštonas
County, in the region of Prienai, Lithuania
ČDM E 5889/a,b

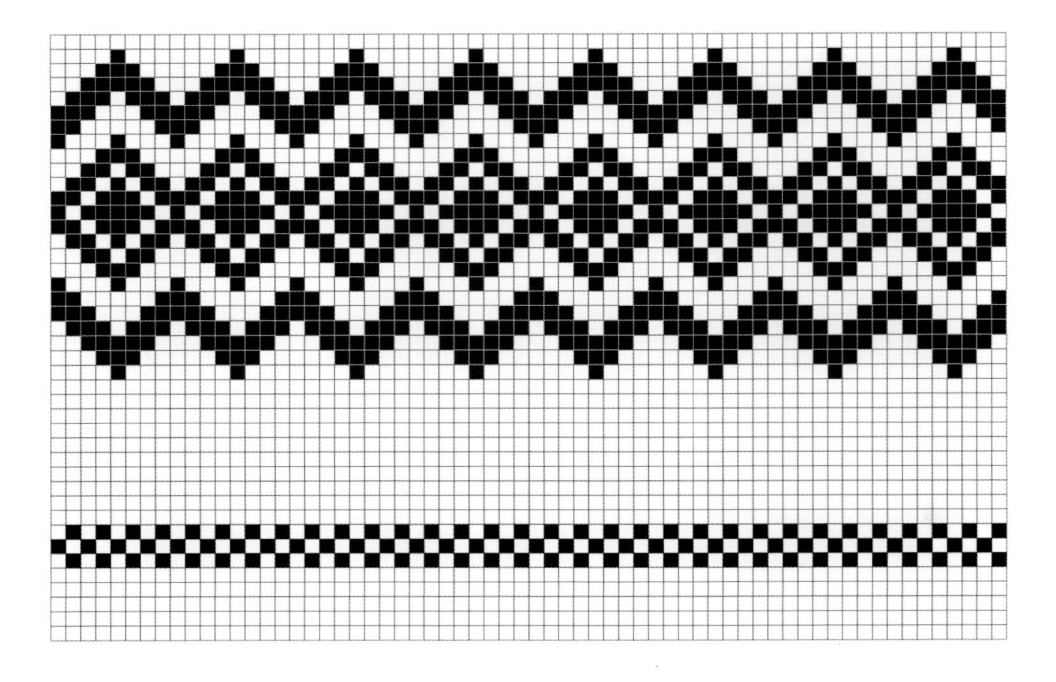

Skill Level: Intermediate
Beads: 1680 white
Other Materials: Yarn in a contrasting color and crochet hook for edging
String half of beads onto yarn. Cast on 40–50 sts for desired length.

Knit all RS rows. On WS rows, work all sts of the bead chart, then knit to the end of the row. Work all rows of chart once. BO, then sew CO and BO edges together. With contrast color, work 1 row of crochet shells (see page 198) around wrist edge.
Make a second wrist warmer the same way.

| **44.** | Dzūkija (Southeastern Lithuania)

45.

Wrist warmers
Made in Nemajūnai County, in the
region of Jieznas, Lithuania
LDM LD 163

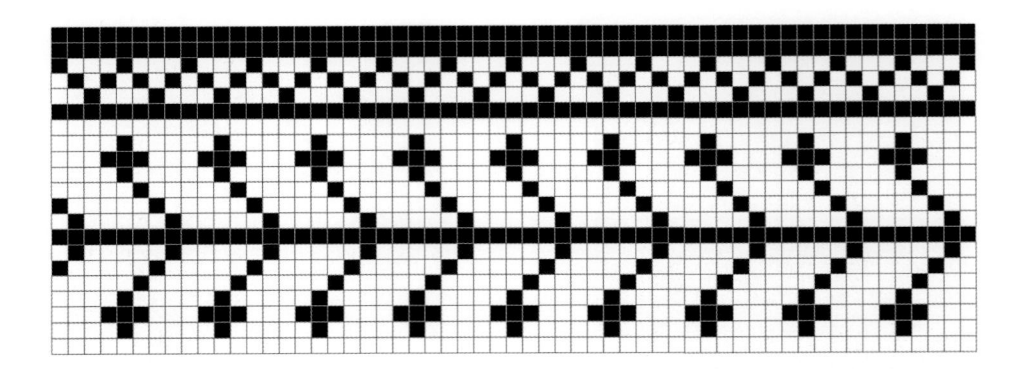

Skill Level: Intermediate
Beads: 1344 color
String half of beads onto yarn. Cast on 40–50 sts for desired length.
Knit all RS rows. On WS rows, work all sts of the bead chart, then knit to the end of the row. Work chart up to last 3 rows, then work 6 more repeats of arrow motif, keeping zigzag pattern lined up as set. BO, then sew CO and BO edges together.
Make a second wrist warmer the same way.

46. Dzūkija (Southeastern Lithuania)

47.

Wrist warmer / *rankovėlė*
Early 20th century
Made in the village of Akmeniai, Kučiūnai County, in the region of Lazdijai, Lithuania
ČDM E 5573

Skill Level: Intermediate
Beads: 1464 white
Other Materials: Additional beads and crochet hook for edging

String half of beads onto yarn. Cast on 40–50 sts for desired length.
Knit all RS rows. On WS rows, work all sts of the bead chart, then knit to the end of the row. Work all rows of chart once, then work one more repeat of pattern. BO, then sew CO and BO edges together.
String some additional beads onto yarn or matching sewing thread. With small crochet hook, work beaded picot edging (see page 198).
Make a second wrist warmer the same way.

| **48.** | DZŪKIJA (SOUTHEASTERN LITHUANIA)

49.

Wrist warmers / *rankankos*
Made in the village of Panarvė,
Šventežeris County, in the region of
Lazdijai, Lithuania
LBM 3696/567/a,b

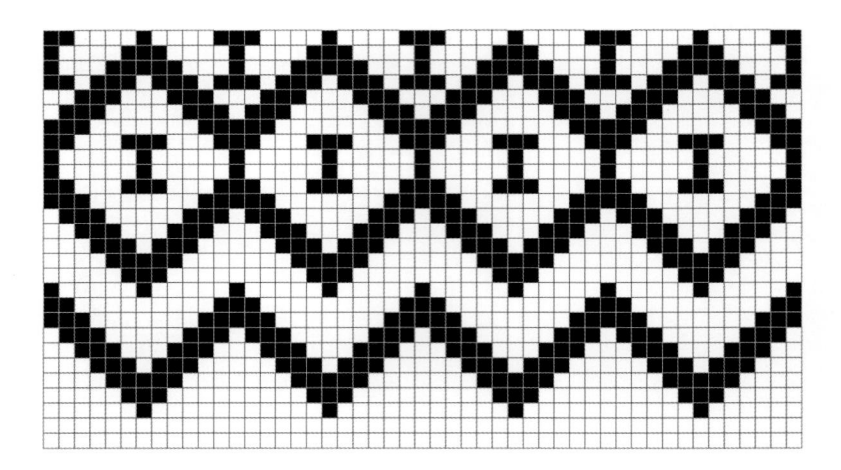

Skill Level: Intermediate
Beads: 1514 white
String half of beads onto yarn. Cast on 40–50 sts for desired length.
Knit all RS rows. On WS rows, work all sts of the bead chart, then knit to the end of the row. Work up to last row of chart, then work two more diamond motifs, ending with last row of chart to match pattern to beginning of piece. BO, then sew CO and BO edges together.
Make a second wrist warmer the same way.

| **50.** | Dzūkija (Southeastern Lithuania)

| 51. |

Wrist warmers
19th century
Made in the village of Buteliūnai, Avižonys County, in the region of Veisiejai, Lithuania
LDM LA 24/a,b.

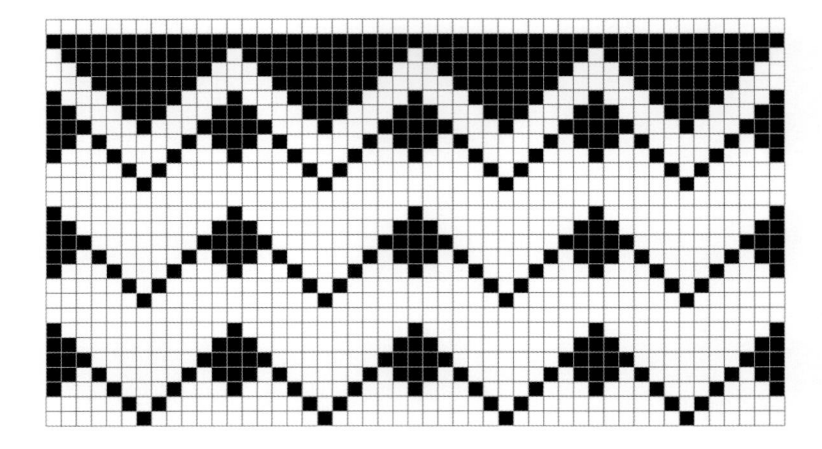

Skill Level: Intermediate
Beads: 1112 white
Other Materials: Additional beads and crochet hook for edging

String half of beads onto yarn. Cast on 40–50 sts for desired length.
Knit all RS rows. On WS rows, work all sts of the bead chart, then knit to the end of the row. Work up to last row of chart, then work two more diamond motifs, ending with last row of chart to match pattern to beginning of piece. BO, then sew CO and BO edges together.
String some additional beads onto yarn or matching sewing thread. With small crochet hook, work beaded picot edging (see page 198).
Make a second wrist warmer the same way.

| **52.** | Dzūkija (Southeastern Lithuania)

53.

Wrist warmers / *rankaukos*
Early 20th century
Made in the village of Krokininkai, Krokialaukis County, in the region of Alytus, Lithuania
LNM EMO 2345/a,b

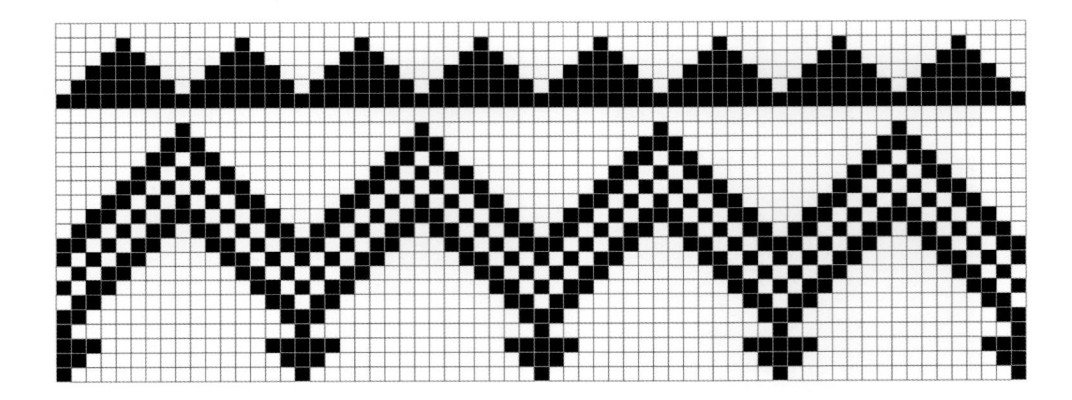

Skill Level: Intermediate
Beads: 994 yellow
Other Materials: Additional beads and crochet hook for edging
String half of beads onto yarn. Cast on 40–50 sts for desired length.
Knit all RS rows. On WS rows, work all sts of the bead chart, then knit to the end of the row. Work up to last row of chart, then work two more diamond motifs, ending with last row of chart to match pattern to beginning of piece. BO, then sew CO and BO edges together.
String some additional beads onto yarn or matching sewing thread. With small crochet hook, work beaded picot edging (see page 198).
Make a second wrist warmer the same way.

| **54.** | DZŪKIJA (SOUTHEASTERN LITHUANIA)

55.

Wrist warmers / *rankafkos*
Late 19th century
Made in the village of Panemunykai, Rumbonys Parish, in the region of Alytus, Lithuania
From the private collection of Dovilė Kulakauskienė

Skill Level: Intermediate
Beads: 2496 white
String half of beads onto yarn. Cast on 40–50 sts for desired length.

Knit all RS rows. On WS rows, work all sts of the bead chart, then knit to the end of the row. Work all rows of chart, then work one more diamond motif. BO, then sew CO and BO edges together.
Make a second wrist warmer the same way.

| **56.** | DZŪKIJA (SOUTHEASTERN LITHUANIA)

| 57. |

Wrist warmers / *rankovėlės*
Early 20th Century
Made in the village of Kalviškiai, Seinai County
(what is now Sejny, Poland)
ČDM E 3870/a,b

Skill Level: Intermediate
Beads: 850 white
Other Materials: Additional beads and crochet hook for edging
String half of beads onto yarn. Cast on 40–50 sts for desired length.
Knit all RS rows. On WS rows, work all sts of the bead chart, then knit to the end of the row. Work all rows of chart once. BO, then sew CO and BO edges together. String additional beads onto yarn or matching sewing thread. With small crochet hook, work beaded picot edging (see page 198).
Make a second wrist warmer the same way.

* Wrist warmer on the right in the photo is from the museum collection.

| **58.** | DZŪKIJA (SOUTHEASTERN LITHUANIA)

59.

Wrist warmers
Made in the village of Čižiūnai, in the area of
Valkininkai, Trakai County, Lithuania
LNM archives, volume 62, page 22
Pattern reproduced by O. D. Aleknienė

Skill Level: Intermediate
Beads: 1200 red
String half of beads onto yarn. Cast on 40–50 sts for desired length.

Knit all RS rows. On WS rows, work all sts of the bead chart, then knit to the end of the row. Work all rows of chart once. BO, then sew CO and BO edges together. Make a second wrist warmer the same way.

| **60.** | Dzūkija (Southeastern Lithuania)

61.

Wrist warmers
19th century
Made in the village of Toliškės, Vilūnai County,
in the region of Kaišiadorys, Lithuania
LDM LA 5238/a,b

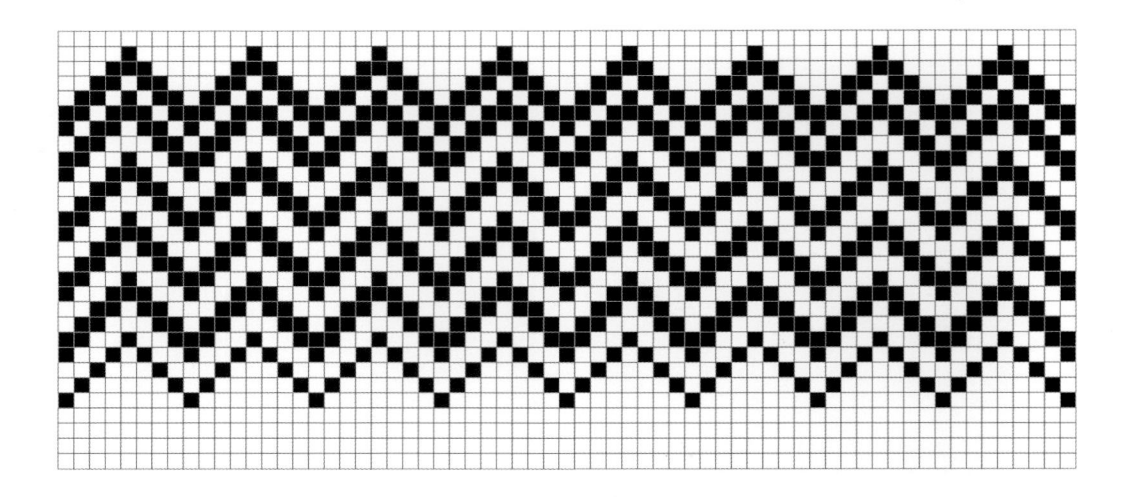

Skill Level: Intermediate
Beads: 1408 white
Other Materials: Crochet hook for edging
String half of beads onto yarn. Cast on 40–50 sts for desired length.
Knit all RS rows. On WS rows, work all sts of the bead chart, then knit to the end of the row. Work all rows of chart once. BO, then sew CO and BO edges together. With small crochet hook, work crochet chain picot edging (see page 198).
Make a second wrist warmer the same way.

| **62.** | DZŪKIJA (SOUTHEASTERN LITHUANIA)

63.

Wrist warmers / *rankaukos*
Late 19th or early 20th century
Made in the village of Užupiai, in the region
of Kaišiadorys, Lithuania
LNM EMO 1855/a,b

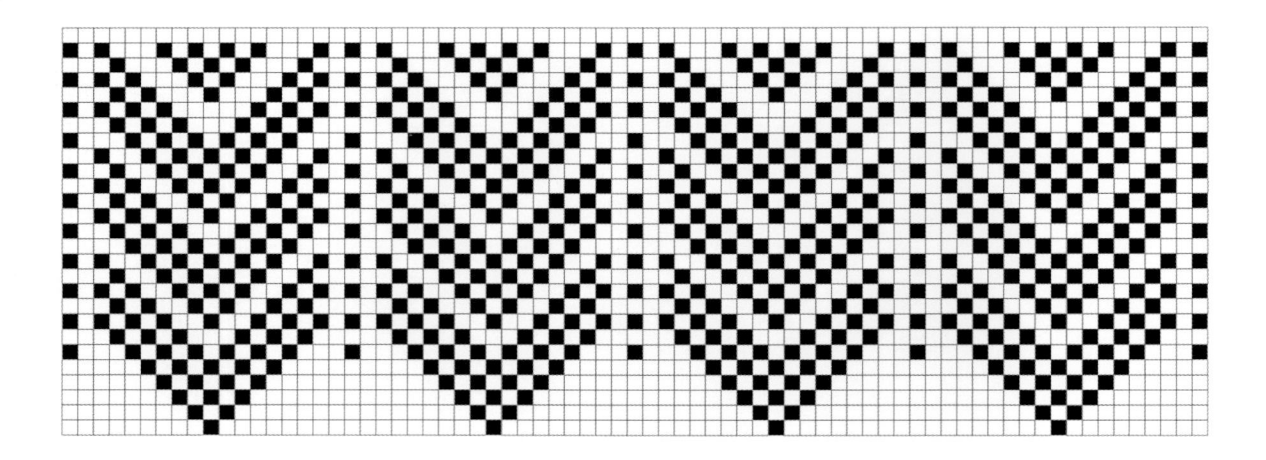

Skill Level: Intermediate
Beads: 1542 white
String half of beads onto yarn. Cast on 40–50 sts for desired length.

Knit all RS rows. On WS rows, work all sts of the bead chart, then knit to the end of the row. Work all rows of chart once. BO, then sew CO and BO edges together. Make a second wrist warmer the same way.

| **64.** | Dzūkija (Southeastern Lithuania)

65.

Wrist warmers / *rankaukos*
Late 19th century
Made in the village of Mokolai, in the region of Marijampolė, Lithuania
MKM GEK 981/a,b

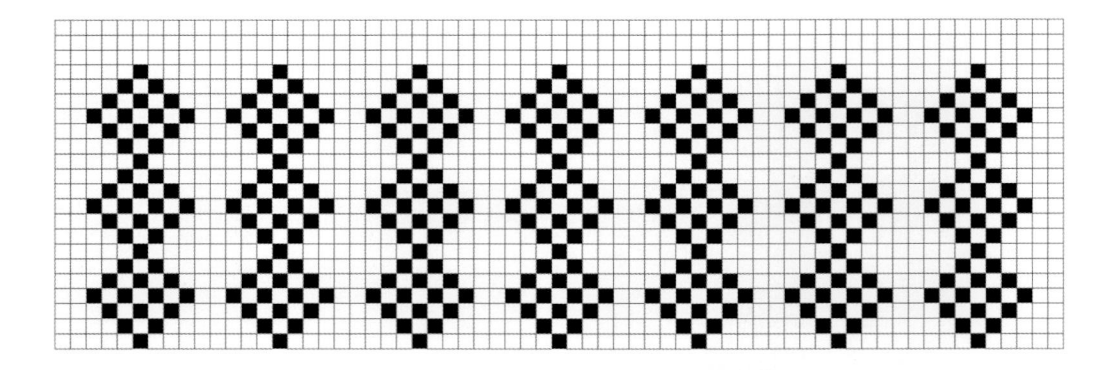

Skill Level: Intermediate
Beads: 644 white
String half of beads onto yarn. Cast on 40–50 sts for desired length.

Knit all RS rows. On WS rows, work all sts of the bead chart, then knit to the end of the row. Work all rows of chart once. BO, then sew CO and BO edges together. Make a second wrist warmer the same way.

| **66.** | SUVALKIJA (SOUTHWESTERN LITHUANIA)

| 67. |

Wrist warmers / *rankovėlės*
Made in Marijampolė, Lithuania
ČDM E 1578/a,b

Skill Level: Intermediate
Beads: 1970 white
String half of beads onto yarn. Cast on 40–50 sts for desired length.
Knit all RS rows. On WS rows, work all sts of the bead chart, then knit to the end of the row. Work up to last 3 rows of chart, then work one more flower/star motif keeping triangle pattern aligned as set and end at center of motif to match beginning of piece. BO, then sew CO and BO edges together.
Make a second wrist warmer the same way.

| **68.** | SUVALKIJA (SOUTHWESTERN LITHUANIA)

69.

Wrist warmers
Late 19th century
Made in the village of Paprūdžiai, Pilviškiai
County, in the region of Vilkaviškis, Lithuania
VKM GEK 1594/a,b

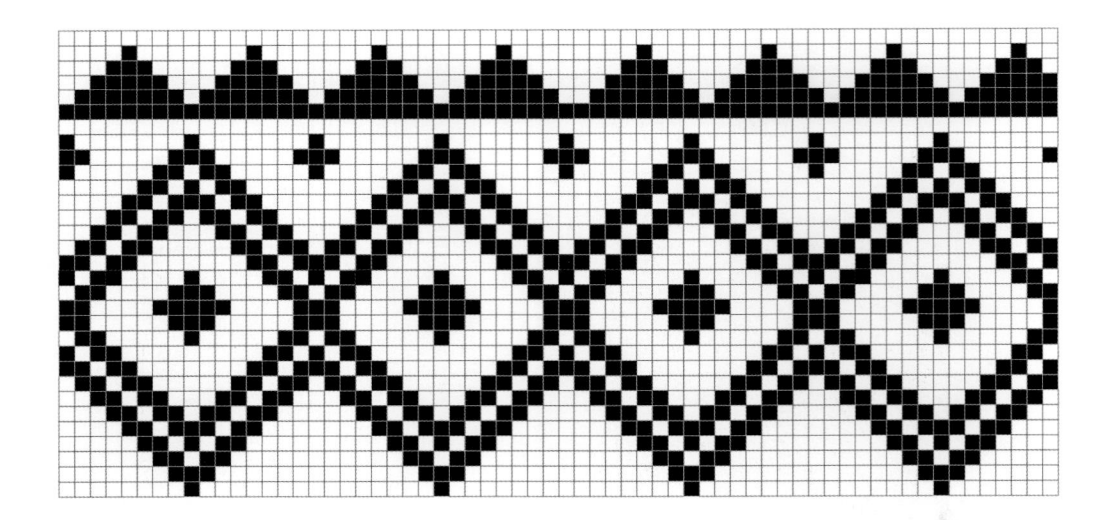

Skill Level: Intermediate
Beads: 1572 white
String half of beads onto yarn. Cast on 40–50 sts for desired length.

Knit all RS rows. On WS rows, work all sts of the bead chart, then knit to the end of the row. Work all rows of chart once. BO, then sew CO and BO edges together. Make a second wrist warmer the same way.

| **70.** | Suvalkija (Southwestern Lithuania)

71.

Wrist warmers / *rankovėlės*
Late 19th century
Made in Vilkaviškis, Lithuania
ČDM E 1545/a,b

Skill Level: Intermediate
Beads: 1232 white
Other Materials: Additional beads and crochet hook for edging
String half of beads onto yarn. Cast on 40–50 sts for desired length.
Knit all RS rows. On WS rows, work all sts of the bead chart, then knit to the end of the row. Work up to last 4 rows of chart, then work one more two more diamond motifs. BO, then sew CO and BO edges together.
String some additional beads onto yarn or matching sewing thread. With small crochet hook, work beaded picot edging (see page 198).
Make a second wrist warmer the same way.

| **72.** | SUVALKIJA (SOUTHWESTERN LITHUANIA)

73.

Wrist warmers / *rankaukos*
Early 20th century
Made in Gižai District, Vilkaviškis
County, Lithuania
LNM EMO 4711/a,b

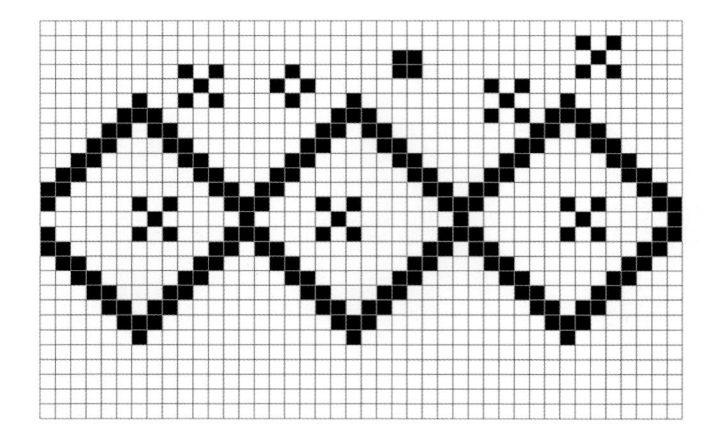

Skill Level: Intermediate
Beads: 900 white
Other Materials: Additional beads and crochet hook for edging
String half of beads onto yarn. Cast on 40–50 sts for desired length.
Knit all RS rows. On WS rows, work all sts of the bead chart, then knit to the end of the row. Work all rows of chart twice. BO, then sew CO and BO edges together. String some additional beads onto yarn or matching sewing thread. With small crochet hook, work beaded picot edging (see page 198).
Make a second wrist warmer the same way.

| **74.** | SUVALKIJA (SOUTHWESTERN LITHUANIA)

75.

Wrist warmers
Made in the village of Šventoji, in the
region of Kretinga, Lithuania
LDM LA 2168/a,b

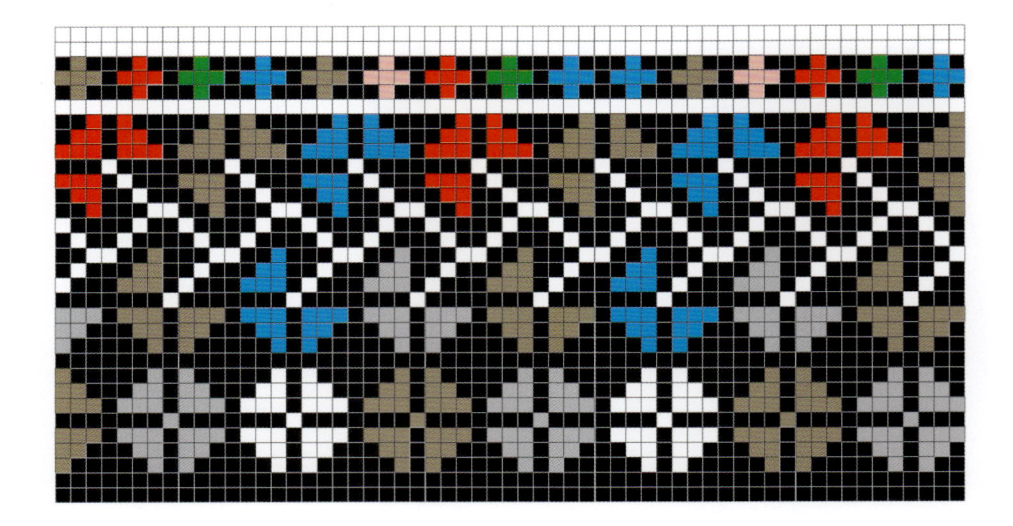

Skill Level: Intermediate
Beads: 120 gray, 240 brown, 680 white, 176 blue, 132 red, 16 pink, 24 green
Other Materials: Additional mixed colors and crochet hook for edging

String beads onto yarn following chart. Cast on 40–50 sts for desired length.

Knit all RS rows. On WS rows, work all sts of the bead chart, then knit to the end of the row. Work all rows of chart once. BO, then sew CO and BO edges together. String some additional beads onto yarn or matching sewing thread. With small crochet hook, work beaded picot edging (see page 198).

Make a second wrist warmer the same way.

| **76.** | Žemaitija (Northwestern Lithuania)

77.

Wrist warmers
Late 19th century
Made in Būtingė, Lithuania
Palanga Traditional Textiles Education Center*

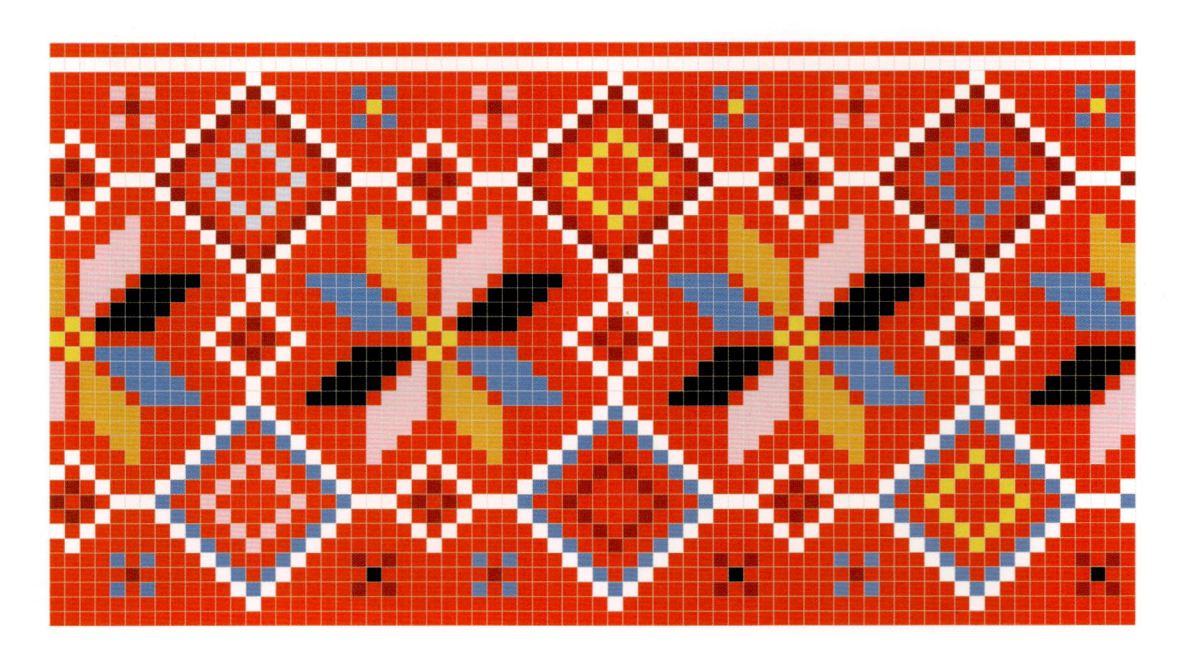

Skill Level: Intermediate
Beads: 378 burgundy, 760 black, 1008 blue, 700 white, 80 yellow, 870 pink, 815 gold
String beads onto yarn following chart. Cast on 40–50 sts for desired length.

Knit all RS rows. On WS rows, work all sts of the bead chart, then knit to the end of the row. Work all rows of chart once. BO, then sew CO and BO edges together. Make a second wrist warmer the same way.

*Photo on the right is from the Palanga Textiles Education Center archives.

| **78.** | ŽEMAITIJA (NORTHWESTERN LITHUANIA)

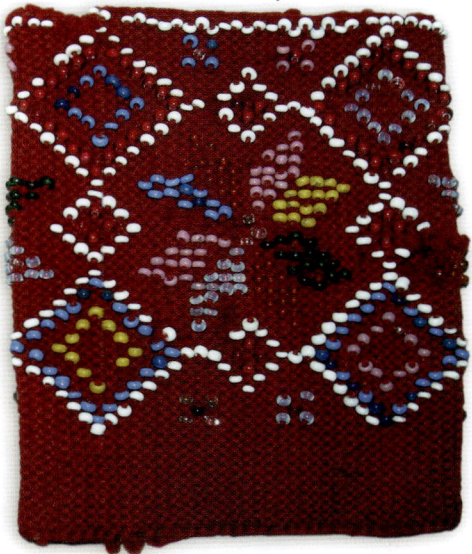

79.

Wrist warmers / *rankaukos*
Made in the village of Maigai, in the region of Mažeikiai County, Mažeikiai County, Lithuania
LDM LA 4261/a,b

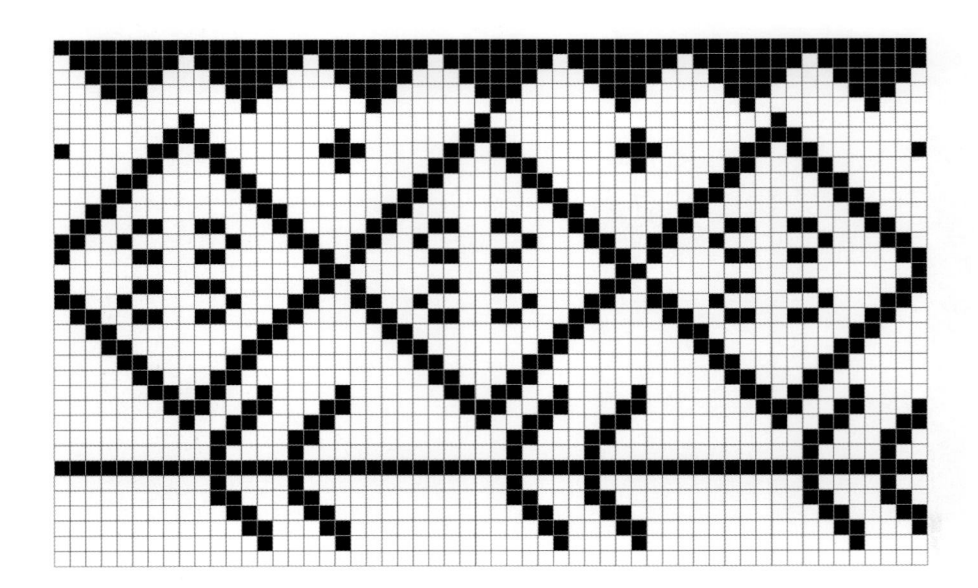

Skill Level: Intermediate
Beads: 1864 white
String half of beads onto yarn. Cast on 40–50 sts for desired length.
Knit all RS rows. On WS rows, work all sts of the bead chart, then knit to the end of the row. Work all rows of chart once, then work one more diamond motif, keeping triangles aligned as set. BO, then sew CO and BO edges together.
Make a second wrist warmer the same way.

| **80.** | Žemaitija (Northwestern Lithuania)

| 81. |

Wrist warmers
Made in the village of Užliekṅė, in the
region of Tirkšliai County, Mažeikiai
County, Lithuania
LDM LA 4685/a,b

Skill Level: Intermediate
Beads: 1968 white
String half of beads onto yarn. Cast on 40–50 sts for desired length.
Knit all RS rows. On WS rows, work all sts of the bead chart, then knit to the end of the row. Work all rows of chart once, then work one more flower/star motif with diamonds below it, keeping zigzag motif aligned as set. BO, then sew CO and BO edges together.
Make a second wrist warmer the same way.

| **82.** | Žemaitija (Northwestern Lithuania)

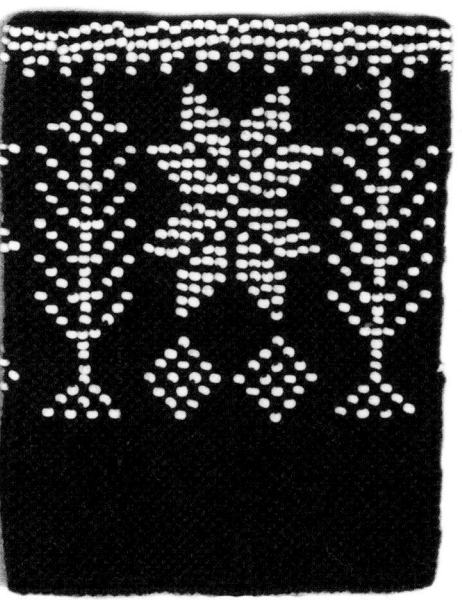

| 83. |

Wrist warmers
Late 19th or early 20th century
Made in the Mažeikiai area, Lithuania
MM E 1480/259

Skill Level: Intermediate
Beads: 1320 white
String half of beads onto yarn. Cast on 40–50 sts for desired length.
Knit all RS rows. On WS rows, work all sts of the bead chart, then knit to the end of the row. Work all rows of chart once, then work one more flower/star motif, continuing line pattern as set. BO, then sew CO and BO edges together.
Make a second wrist warmer the same way.

| **84.** | Žemaitija (Northwestern Lithuania)

85.

Wrist warmers
19th century
Made in the village of Latakai, Viduklė
District, Raseiniai County, Lithuania
ŠAM EO 455/a,b

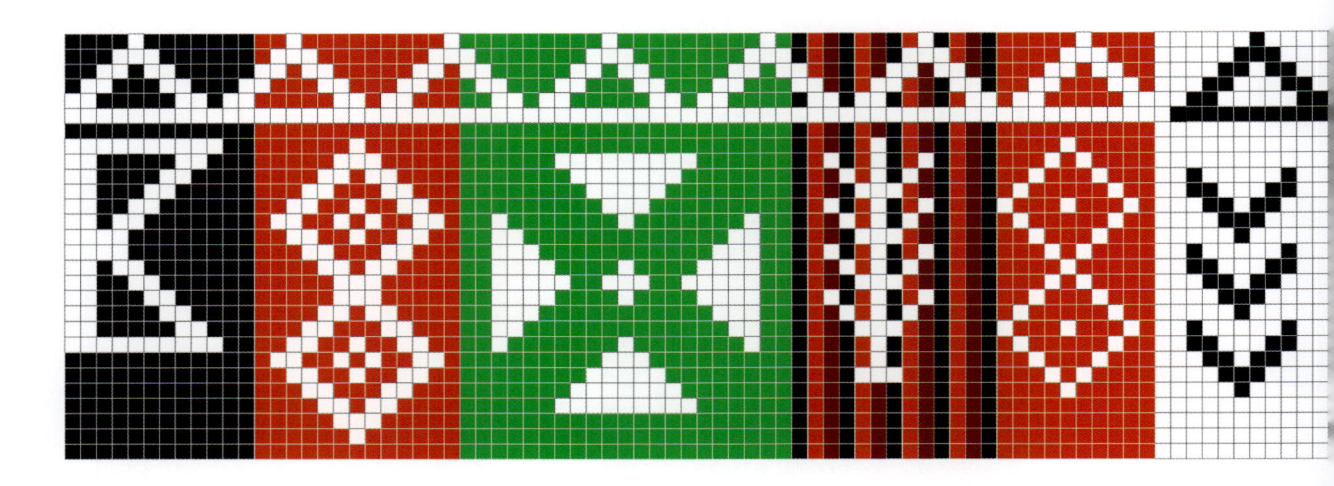

Skill Level: Experienced
Beads: 2264 white
Yarn Colors: Red, black, and green
String half of beads onto green yarn, and one-quarter on each of black and red yarn. Cast on 40–50 sts for desired length.

Knit all RS rows, changing colors as charted or as desired. Change colors on WS (bead) rows. On WS rows, work all sts of the bead chart, then knit to the end of the row. Work all rows of chart, then work one more diamond motif. BO, then sew CO and BO edges together.
Make a second wrist warmer the same way.

| **86.** | ŽEMAITIJA (NORTHWESTERN LITHUANIA)

87.

Wrist warmers / *rankelkos*
19th century
Made in the village of Latakai, Viduklė
District, Raseiniai County, Lithuania
ŠAM EO 456/a,b

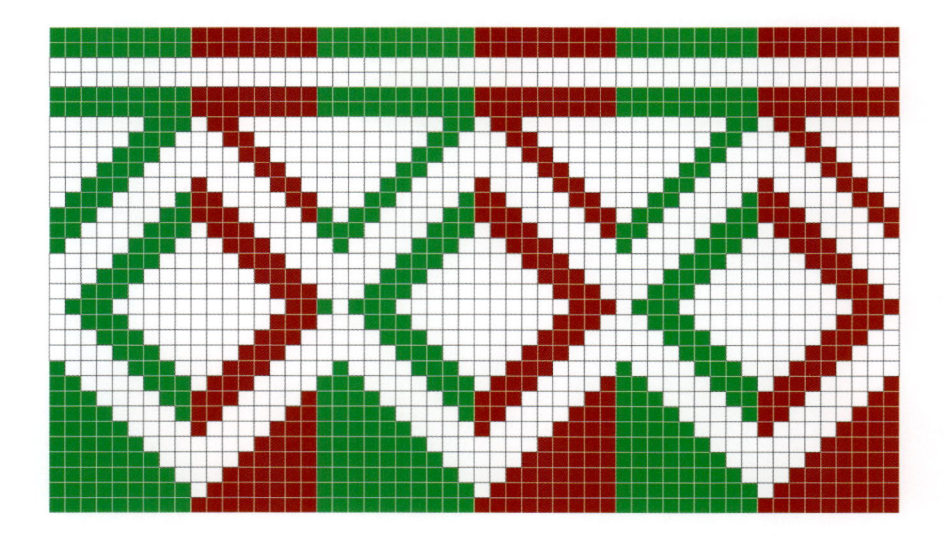

Skill Level: Experienced
Beads: 2264 white
Yarn Colors: Red and green
String half of beads onto each color of yarn. Cast on 40–50 sts for desired length.

Knit all RS rows. Change colors as charted on WS (bead) rows. On WS rows, work all sts of the bead chart, then knit to the end of the row. Work all rows of chart once, then work one more diamond repeat. BO, then sew CO and BO edges together.
Make a second wrist warmer the same way.

| **88.** | Žemaitija (Northwestern Lithuania)

89.

Wrist warmer
Made in Rietavas, in the region of
Plungė County, Lithuania
LDM LA 4479

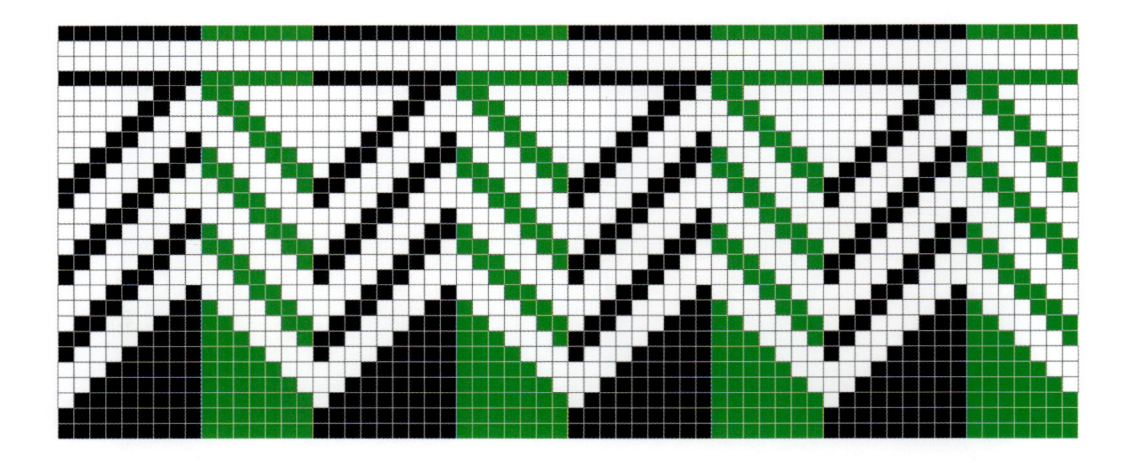

Skill Level: Experienced
Beads: 1560 white
Yarn Colors: Black and green
String half of beads onto each color of yarn. Cast on 40–50 sts for desired length.

Knit all RS rows. Change colors as charted on WS (bead) rows. On WS rows, work all sts of the bead chart, then knit to the end of the row. Work all rows of chart once. BO, then sew CO and BO edges together. Make a second wrist warmer the same way.

| **90.** | Žemaitija (Northwestern Lithuania)

91.

Wrist warmers / *mankietai*
Early 20th century
Made in the village of Meškiai, Šiaudinė
County, in the region of Akmenė, Lithuania
LDM LA 1353/a,b

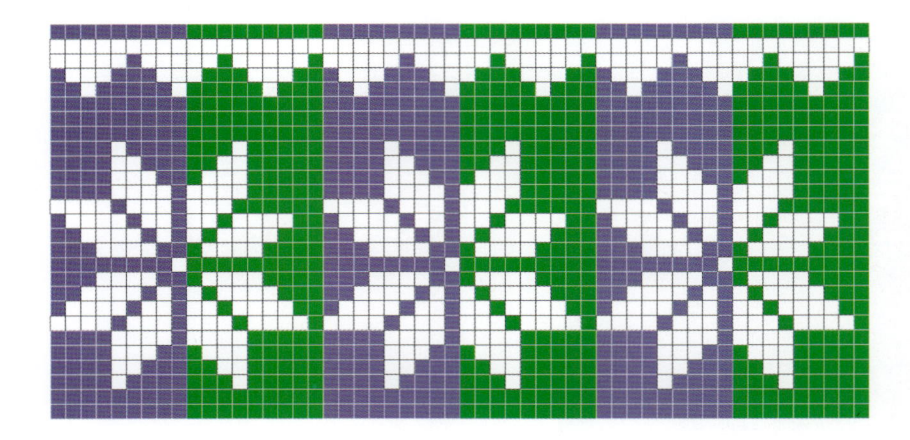

Skill Level: Experienced
Beads: 1038 white
Yarn Colors: Blue and green
String half of beads onto each color of yarn. Cast on 40–50 sts for desired length.

Knit all RS rows. Change colors as charted on RS (plain) rows. On WS rows, work all sts of the bead chart, then knit to the end of the row. Work all rows of chart once. BO, then sew CO and BO edges together.
Make a second wrist warmer the same way.

| **92.** | Žemaitija (Northwestern Lithuania)

93.

Wrist warmers / *rankelkos*
Late 19th century
Made in Pagramantis, in the region of
Tauragė, Lithuania
LNM EMO 1883/a,b

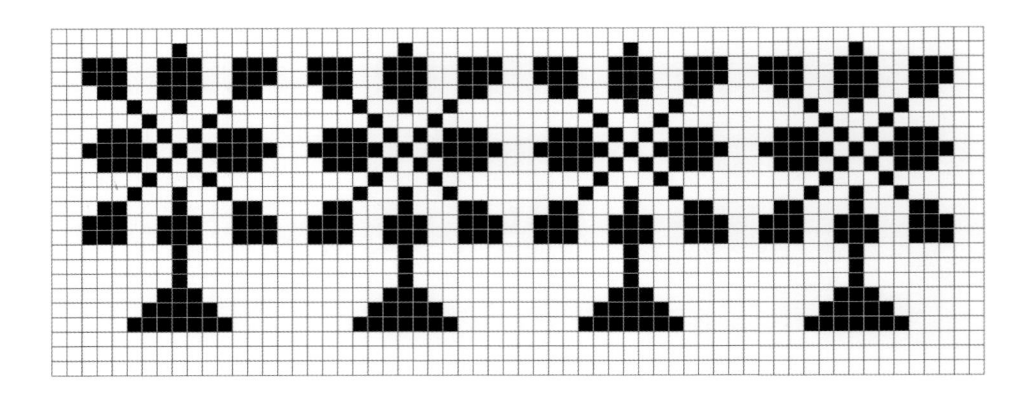

Skill Level: Intermediate
Beads: 832 white
Other Materials: Additional beads and crochet hook for edging
String half of beads onto yarn. Cast on 40–50 sts for desired length.
Knit all RS rows. On WS rows, work all sts of the bead chart, then knit to the end of the row. Work all rows of chart once. BO, then sew CO and BO edges together. String some additional beads onto yarn or matching sewing thread. With small crochet hook, work beaded picot edging (see page 198).
Make a second wrist warmer the same way.

| **94.** | ŽEMAITIJA (NORTHWESTERN LITHUANIA)

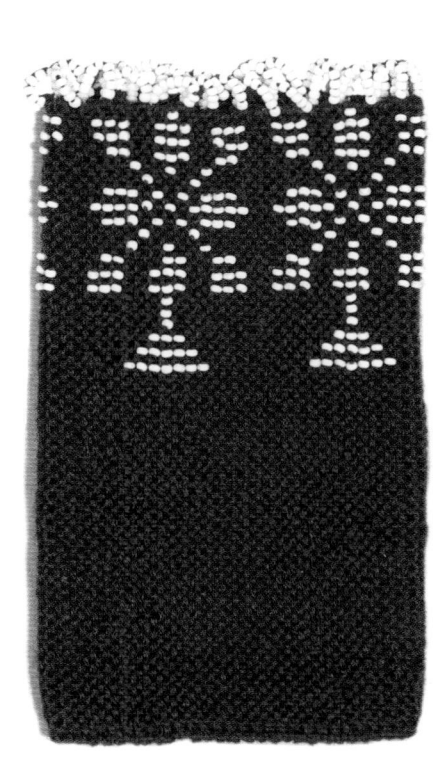

95.

Wrist warmers / *rankelkos*
Early 20th century
Made in the village of Vaitimėnai, Mažonai County,
in the region of Tauragė, Lithuania
Upyna Folk Art Museum (Šilalė county)
Exhibit nos. 1061 and 1062

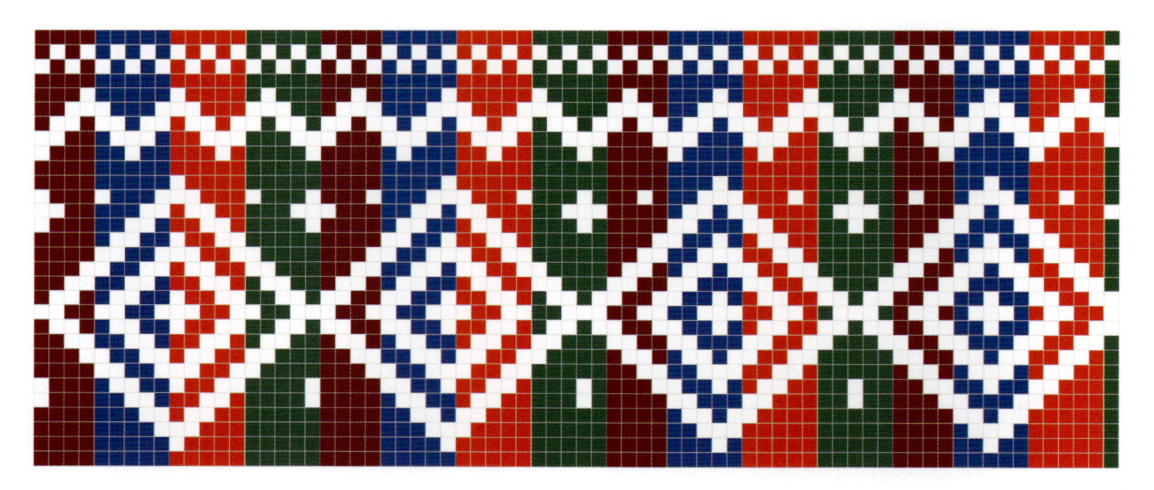

Skill Level: Experienced
Beads: 1280 white
Yarn Colors: Red, blue, burgundy, and green
String one-quarter of beads onto each color of yarn. Cast on 40–50 sts for desired length.

Knit all RS rows. Change colors as charted on RS (plain) rows. On WS rows, work all sts of the bead chart, then knit to the end of the row. Work all rows of chart once. BO, then sew CO and BO edges together.
Make a second wrist warmer the same way.

| **96.** | Žemaitija (Northwestern Lithuania)

97.

Men's wrist warmers
Made in the region of Kelmė,
Lithuania
LNM EMO 4251/a,b

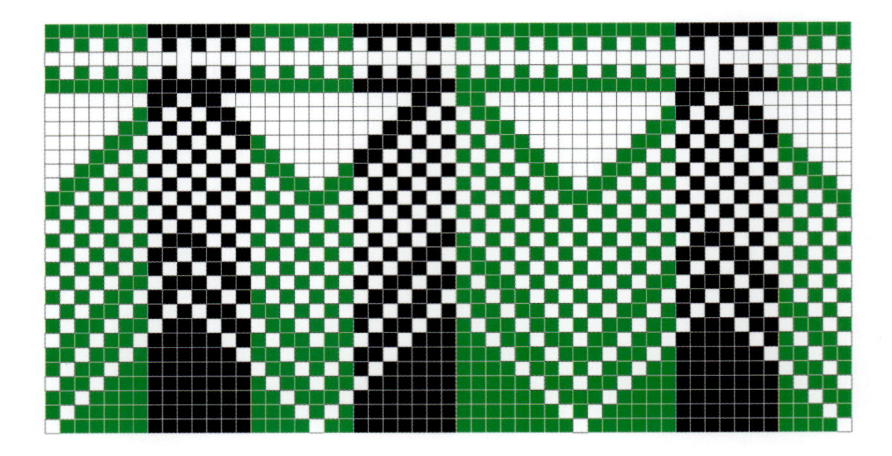

Skill Level: Experienced
Beads: 1266 white
Yarn Colors: Black and green
String half of beads onto each color of yarn. Cast on 40–50 sts for desired length.
Knit all RS rows. Change color as charted or after every 8 rows as shown on sample. Change colors on WS (beaded) rows. On WS rows, work all sts of the bead chart, then knit to the end of the row. Work all rows of chart once. BO, then sew CO and BO edges together. Make a second wrist warmer the same way.

| **98.** | ŽEMAITIJA (NORTHWESTERN LITHUANIA)

| **99.** |

Men's wrist warmers / *rankovėčiai*
Late 19th century
Made in the village of Kumžaičiai, Kuliai
County, in the region of Plungė, Lithuania
LNM EMO 2347/a,b

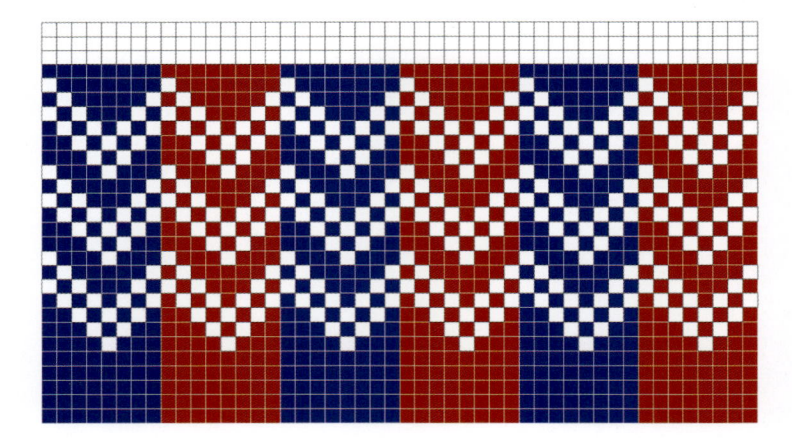

Skill Level: Experienced
Beads: 1152 white
Yarn Colors: Red and blue
String half of beads onto each color of yarn. Cast on 40–50 sts for desired length.
Knit all RS rows. Change colors as charted on RS (plain) rows. On WS rows, work all sts of the bead chart, then knit to the end of the row. Work all rows of chart once, then work one more repeat of red and blue sections. BO, then sew CO and BO edges together.
Make a second wrist warmer the same way.

| **100.** | Žemaitija (Northwestern Lithuania)

| **101.** |

Wrist warmers / *rankelkos*
19th century
Made in Ylakiai, in the region of
Skuodo, Lithuania
LDM LD 767/a,b

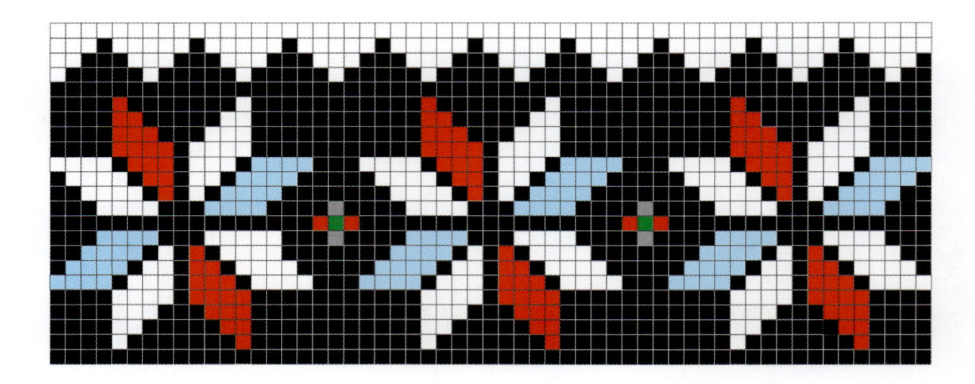

Skill Level: Intermediate
Beads: 672 white, 192 blue, 204 red, 8 gray, 4 green
String beads onto yarn following chart. Cast on 40–50 sts for desired length.

Knit all RS rows. On WS rows, work all sts of the bead chart, then knit to the end of the row. Work all rows of chart once. BO, then sew CO and BO edges together. Make a second wrist warmer the same way.

| **102.** | Žemaitija (Northwestern Lithuania)

103.

Wrist warmers / *rukavičnikai*
Early 20th century
Made in the village of Dilbikiai, Ylakiai County,
in the region of Skuodo, Lithuania
From the private collection of Asta Miltenytė

Skill Level: Intermediate
Beads: 1264 white
String half of beads onto yarn. Cast on 40–50 sts for desired length.

Knit all RS rows. On WS rows, work all sts of the bead chart, then knit to the end of the row. Work all rows of chart once. BO, then sew CO and BO edges together. Make a second wrist warmer the same way.

| **104.** | Žemaitija (Northwestern Lithuania)

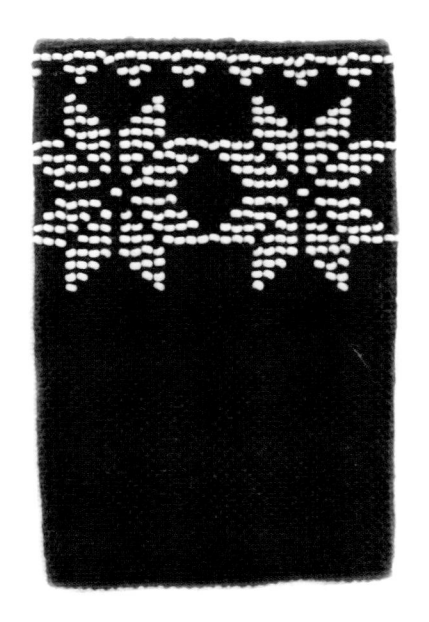

105.

Wrist warmers / *rukavičnikai*
Early 20th century
Made in Ylakiai, in the region of Skuodo, Lithuania
From the private collection of Asta Miltenytė

Skill Level: Intermediate
Beads: 1544 white
String half of beads onto yarn. Cast on 40–50 sts for desired length.

Knit all RS rows. On WS rows, work all sts of the bead chart, then knit to the end of the row. Work all rows of chart once. BO, then sew CO and BO edges together. Make a second wrist warmer the same way.

| **106.** | ŽEMAITIJA (NORTHWESTERN LITHUANIA)

107.

Wrist warmers / *rankelkos*
Made in the village of Papaukštkalnis, Upyna County, in the region of Šilalė, Lithuania
LNM EMO 8600/a,b

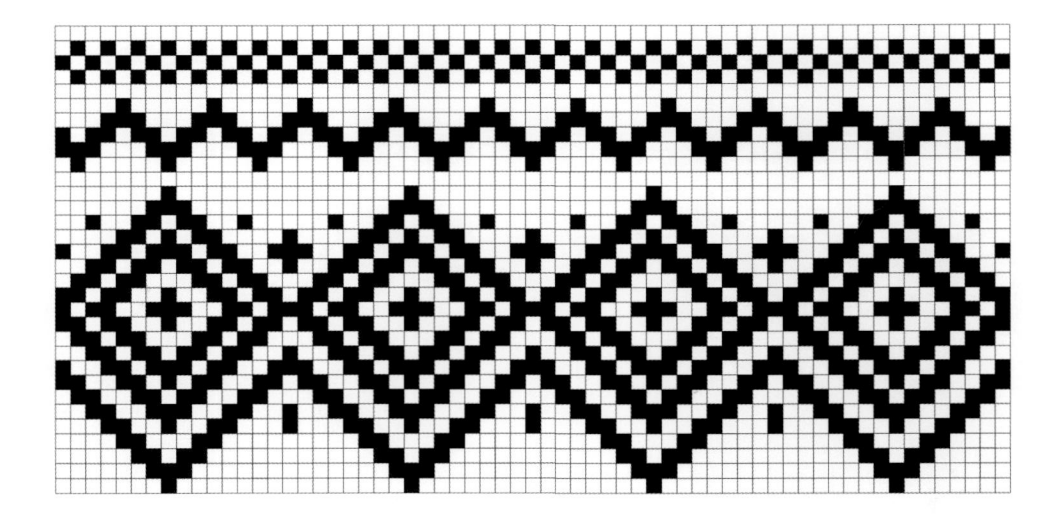

Skill Level: Intermediate
Beads: 1184 white
String half of beads onto yarn. Cast on 40–50 sts for desired length.

Knit all RS rows. On WS rows, work all sts of the bead chart, then knit to the end of the row. Work all rows of chart once. BO, then sew CO and BO edges together. Make a second wrist warmer the same way.

| **108.** | ŽEMAITIJA (NORTHWESTERN LITHUANIA)

109.

Wrist warmers / *rankelkos*
Early 20th century
Made in the village of Lingiai, Upyna County,
in the region of Šilalė, Lithuania
Upyna Folk Art Museum (Šilalė county)
Exhibit nos. 2225 and 2226

Skill Level: Intermediate
Beads: 630 white
String half of beads onto yarn. Cast on 40–50 sts for desired length.

Knit all RS rows. On WS rows, work all sts of the bead chart, then knit to the end of the row. Work all rows of chart once. BO, then sew CO and BO edges together. Make a second wrist warmer the same way.

| **110.** | Žemaitija (Northwestern Lithuania)

| **111.** |

Wrist warmers
Made in Tryškiai, in the region of
Telšiai, Lithuania.
LDM LS 274/a,b

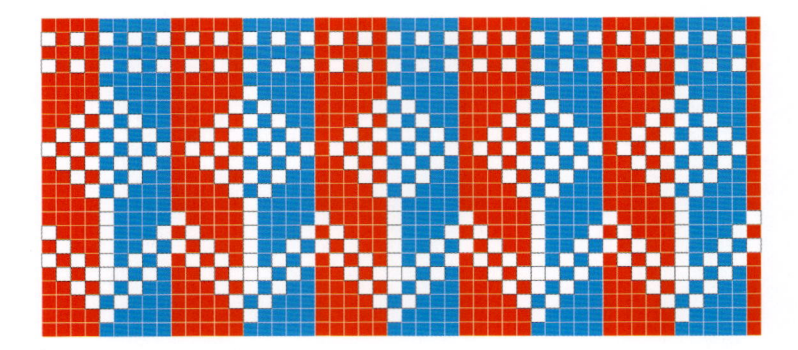

Skill Level: Experienced
Beads: 994 white
Yarn Colors: Red and blue
String half of beads onto each color of yarn. Cast on 40–50 sts for desired length.
Knit all RS rows. Change colors as charted on RS (plain) rows. On WS rows, work all sts of the bead chart, then knit to the end of the row. Work all rows of chart once, then start chart over and work the first 19 rows once more. BO, then sew CO and BO edges together.
Make a second wrist warmer the same way.

| **112.** | Žemaitija (Northwestern Lithuania)

113.

Wrist warmers
Made in Tryškiai, in the region of
Telšiai, Lithuania
LDM LS 275/a,b

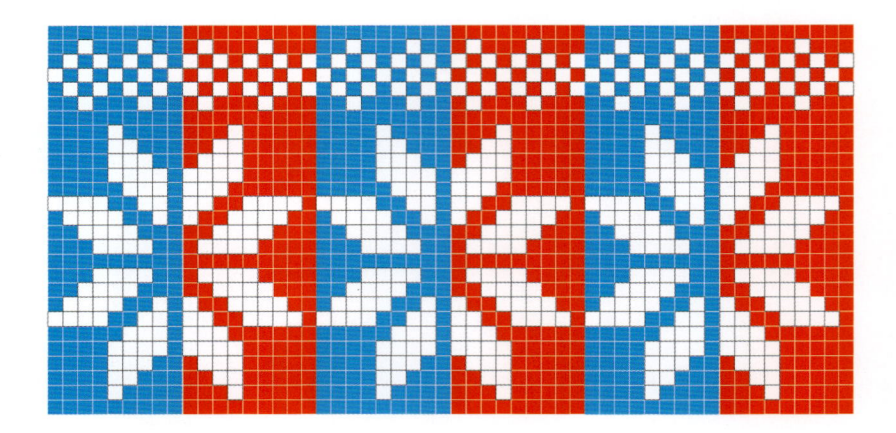

Skill Level: Experienced
Beads: 1344 white
Yarn Colors: Red and blue
String half of beads onto each color of yarn. Cast on 40–50 sts for desired length.
Knit all RS rows. Change colors as charted on RS (plain) rows. On WS rows, work all sts of the bead chart, then knit to the end of the row. Work all rows of chart once, then work one more flower/star motif (read and blue section), keeping diamonds aligned as set. BO, then sew CO and BO edges together.
Make a second wrist warmer the same way.

| **114.** | ŽEMAITIJA (NORTHWESTERN LITHUANIA)

115.

Wrist warmers / *maukos*
Made in Nemirseta, Klaipėda County, Lithuania
From "Lietuvininkų pirštinės" ("The Gloves of Lithuania Minor") by Irena Regina Merkienė and Marija Pautieniūtė–Banionienė. *Lietuvos etnologija.* (Lithuanian Ethnology) vol 3, Vilnius: Žara. 1998, pg. 191.

Skill Level: Intermediate
Beads: 756 white

String half of beads onto yarn. Cast on 40–50 sts for desired length.

Knit all RS rows. On WS rows, work all sts of the bead chart, then knit to the end of the row. Work all rows of chart once. BO, then sew CO and BO edges together. Make a second wrist warmer the same way.

| 116. | Klaipeda Area

| 117. |

Wrist warmers / *rankelkos*
ŠAM EO 457

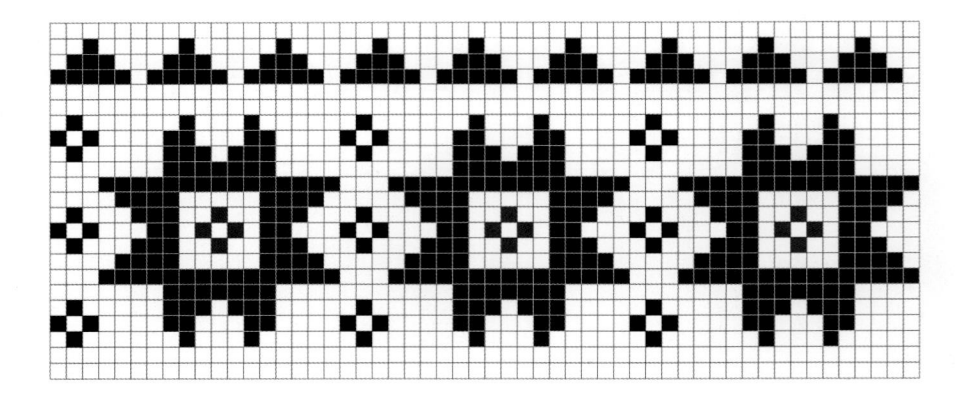

Skill Level: Intermediate
Beads: 824 white
String half of beads onto yarn. Cast on 40–50 sts for desired length.
Knit all RS rows. On WS rows, work all sts of the bead chart, then knit to the end of the row. Work all rows of chart once, then work one more repeat of star pattern with small diamonds. BO, then sew CO and BO edges together.
Make a second wrist warmer the same way.

| **118.** | Origin Unknown

119.

Wrist warmers / *rankovička*
Early 20th century
ČDM E 1574

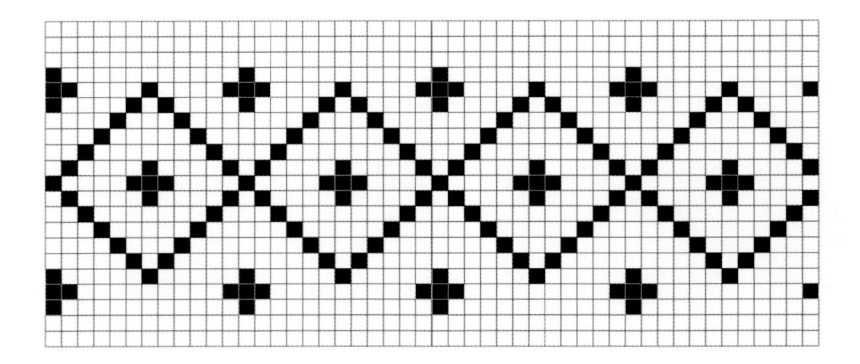

Skill Level: Intermediate
Beads: 390 white
String half of beads onto yarn. Cast on 40–50 sts for desired length.

Knit all RS rows. On WS rows, work all sts of the bead chart, then knit to the end of the row. Work all rows of chart once, then work two more diamond repeats. BO, then sew CO and BO edges together.
Make a second wrist warmer the same way.

| **120.** | Origin Unknown

121.

Wrist warmers / *runkaukos*
From *Lietuvių tautiniai drabužiai* (Lithuanian National Costume) by M. Glemžaitė. Vilnius. 1955, pg. 55.

Skill Level: Intermediate
Beads: 1110 white
String half of beads onto yarn. Cast on 40–50 sts for desired length.

Knit all RS rows. On WS rows, work all sts of the bead chart, then knit to the end of the row. Work all rows of chart once. BO, then sew CO and BO edges together. Make a second wrist warmer the same way.

| **122.** | ORIGIN UNKNOWN

123.

Glove
National M.K. Čiurlionis Museum of Fine Arts

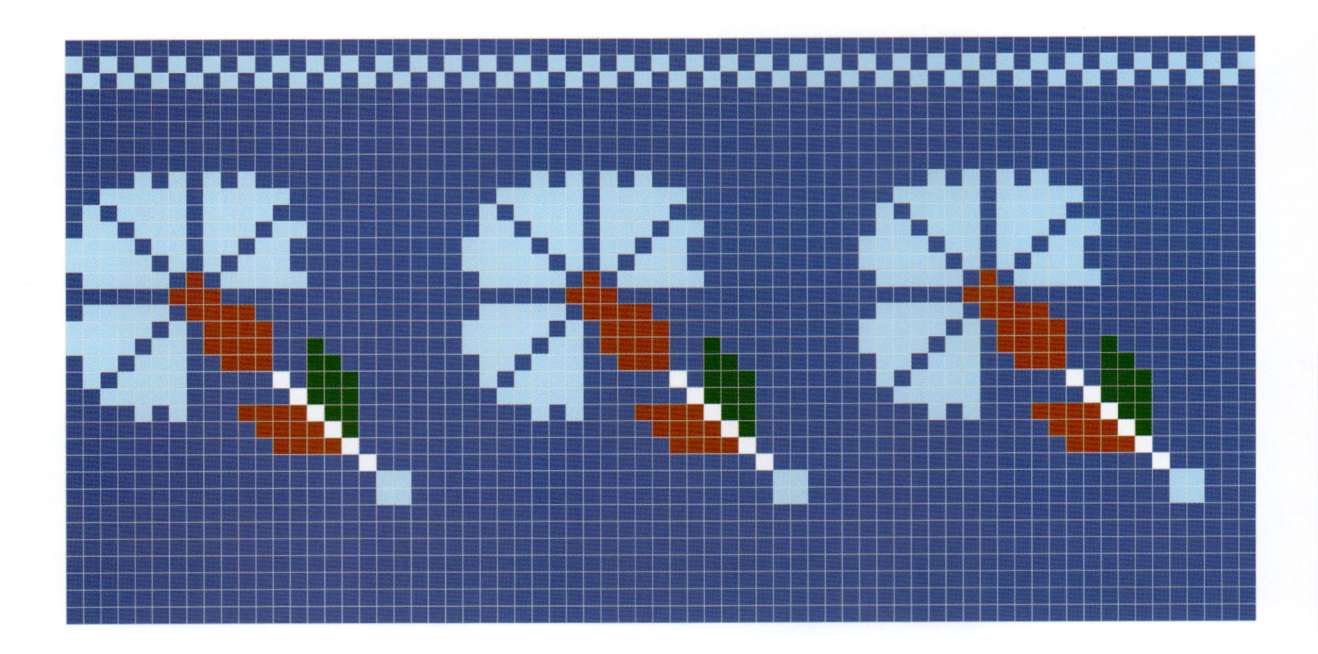

Skill Level: Intermediate
Beads: 675 blue, 36 white, 126 red, 72 green
String beads onto yarn following chart. Cast on 40–50 sts for desired length.

Knit all RS rows. On WS rows, work all sts of the bead chart, then knit to the end of the row. Work all rows of chart once. BO, then sew CO and BO edges together. Make a second wrist warmer the same way.

| **124.** | Origin Unknown

125.

Wrist warmers
Origin unknown
From the private collection of Lucija Dobrickienė.

Skill Level: Intermediate
Beads: 1540 silver or gray
String half of beads onto yarn. Cast on 40–50 sts for desired length.

Knit all RS rows. On WS rows, work all sts of the bead chart, then knit to the end of the row. Work all rows of chart once. BO, then sew CO and BO edges together. Make a second wrist warmer the same way.

126. | ORIGIN UNKNOWN

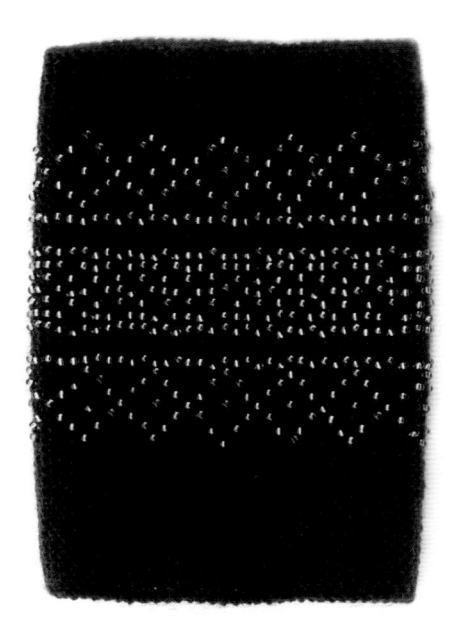

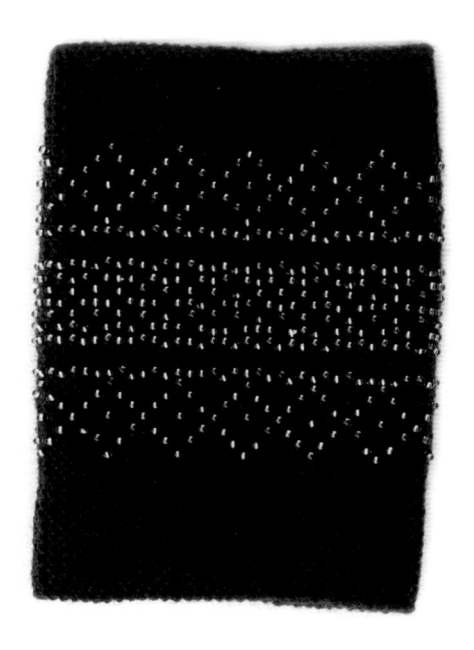

127.

Gloves
PKM GEK 2719/E100

Skill Level: Intermediate
Beads: 1050 white
String half of beads onto yarn. Cast on 40–50 sts for desired length.
Knit all RS rows. On WS rows, work all sts of the bead chart, then knit to the end of the row. Work all rows of chart once, then work one more repeat of both tree motifs ending with plain rows. BO, then sew CO and BO edges together.
Make a second wrist warmer the same way.

| **128.** | Origin Unknown

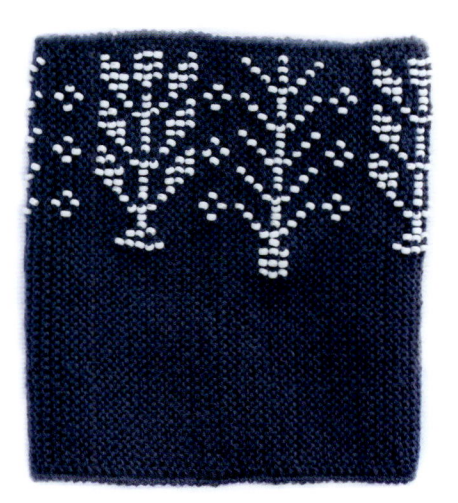

APPENDIX I:
OTHER WOOL WRIST WARMERS IN MUSEUM COLLECTIONS
AUKŠTAITIJA (NORTHEASTERN LITHUANIA)

| 1. |

Wrist warmers
Late 19th century
Made in the town of Pabiržė, Biržai County, Lithuania
ČDM E 1541/a, b

| 2. |

Wrist Warmers / *rankovėlės*
Late 19th or early 20th century
Made in the village of Latveliai, Nemunėlio Radviliškis District, in the region of Biržai, Lithuania
ČDM E 1540/a, b

| 3. |

Wrist warmers
Late 19th or early 20th century
Made in Pasvalys, Biržai County, Lithuania
ČDM E 1542 /a, b

| 4. |

Glove
Early 20th century
Made in the village of Liepiškiai, Šiaulėnai District, Šiauliai County, Lithuania
ČDM E 1557

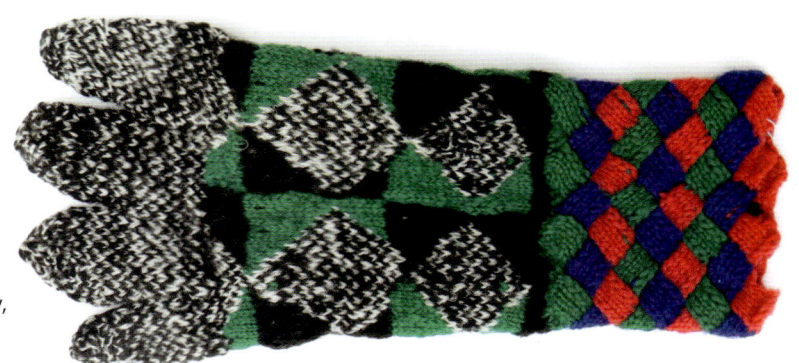

| 5. |

Wrist warmers
Late 19th or early 20th century
Made in Pasvalys, Biržai County, Lithuania
ČDM E 1548/a, b

| Dzūkija (Southeastern Lithuania) |

| 7. |

Wrist warmer
Made in the town of Meteliai,
Seirijai District, Alytus County,
Lithuania
ŠAM EO 625

| 6. |

Wrist warmer
Late 19th or early 20th century
Made in the vicinity of Kančėnai,
Daugai County, in the region of
Alytaus, Lithuania
LDM LA 1123

| 8. |

Wrist warmers
Made in the village of Cigoniškiai,
Parečėnų County, in the region of
Alytaus, Lithuania
LBM 3712/568/a, b

| **9.** |

Wrist warmers/knitted cuffs
Made in the village of Miežoniai,
Palomenės County, in the region
of Kaišiadoris, Lithuania
From the Kaišiadorius Museum
collection.

| **10.** |

Wrist warmers
Made in the village of Avižieniai,
Šlavantai County, in the region of
Lazdijai, Lithuania
LNM EMO 5559/a, b

| 11. |

Wrist warmer
Made in the village of Čižiūnai,
Aukštadvaris District, Trakai County,
Lithuania
Anastazija and Antanas Tamošaičiai
Gallery "Židinys," exhibit no. 230

| 12. |

Wrist warmers
Early 20th century
Made in the village of Kristapiškiai,
Lelioniai County, in the region of Prienai,
Lithuania
ČDM E 3397/a, b

| 13. |

Wrist warmer
Early 20th century
Made in the village of Kružiūnai,
Balbieriškis County, in the region
of Prienai, Lithuania
LNM EMO 3893

| 14. |

Wrist warmers
20th century
Made in the village of Kunigiškiai,
Balbieriškis County, in the region
of Prienai, Lithuania
LDM LA 4107/a, b

| 15. |

Wrist warmers
Late 19th or early 20th century
Knit in ribbing with bead embroidery
Made in Druskininkai, Lithuania
LBM P-206/a, b

| Suvalkija (Southwestern Lithuania) |

| 16. |

Wrist warmers
Late 19th century
Made in the village of Tarpučiai, Šunskai
County, in the region of Marijampolė,
Lithuania
MKM GEK Nr.982/a, b

| 17. |

Wrist warmers
Early 20th century
Made in the village of Trakiškiai, Trakiškiai
County, in the region of Marijampolė,
Lithuania
MKM GEK 983/a, b

| 18. |

Wrist warmers
Early 20th century
Made in the village of Trakiškiai, Trakiškiai County, in the region of Marijampolė, Lithuania
MKM GEK Nr.984/a, b

| 19. |

Wrist warmers
Early 20th century
Made in Šunskai, Šunskai County, in the region of Marijampolė, Lithuania
LDM LA 2190/a, b

| 20. |

Wrist warmers
Late 19th century
Made in Šunskai, Šunskai County, in the region of Marijampolė, Lithuania
LDM LA 2191/a, b

| 21. |

Wrist warmers
Early 20th century
Made in the village of Daukšiai, Padovinis County, in the region of Marijampolė, Lithuania
LDM LA 2207/a, b

| 22. |

Wrist warmers
Late 19th to early 20th century
Made in the village of Turlojiškė,
Naujiena County, in the region of
Marijampolė, Lithuania
LDM LA 2935 /a, b

| 24. |

Wrist warmer
Late 19th to early 20th century
Made in the village of Viliušiai,
Jankai County, in the region of
Šakių, Lithuania
LNM EMO 5558

| 23. |

Wrist warmer
Late 19th to early 20th century
Made in the region of Marijampolė,
Lithuania
LNM EMO 7383

| **25.** |

Wrist warmer
Made in Šakiai County, Lithuania
ČDM E 2410/a, b

| **26.** |

Wrist warmer
Made in the village of Varčiuliai, Kiduliai
District, Šakiai County, Lithuania
Anastazija and Antanas Tamošaičiai Gallery
"Židinys". Exibit no. 231

| **27.** |

Wrist warmers
Made in Pilviškiai, Pilviškiai County,
in the region of Vilkaviškis, Lithuania
LNM EMO 7467/a, b

28.

Wrist warmers
Late 19th or early 20th century
Made in Suvalkija, Lithuania
LNM EMO 9082/a, b
Right side (top), wrong side (bottom)

| Žemaitija (Northwestern Lithuania) |

| 29. |

Wrist warmers
Early 20th century
Made in Viekšniai, in the region of
Akmenė, Lithuania
MM GEK 1479 E 258/a, b

| 30. |

Women's wrist warmer
Early 20th century
Made in Palanga, Lithuania
LNM EMO 3042

| **31.** |

Wrist warmers
Made in Palanga, Lithuania
Palanga Traditional Textiles
Education Center

| **32.** |

Wrist warmers
Made in Palanga, Lithuania
Palanga Traditional Textiles
Education Center

| 33. |

Wrist warmers with button closure
Late 19th to early 20th century
Made in Kalvarija, Žemaičiai County, in the region of Plungė, Lithuania
ŽMA GEK 12.223 /a, b

| 34. |

Wrist warmers
Early 20th century
Made in Kelmė, Raseiniai County, Lithuania
ŠAM EO 639/a, b

| 35. |

Wrist warmer
Early 20th century
Made in the village of Graužai, Viduklė District, Raseiniai County, Lithuania
ŠAM EO 625/1

| **36.** |

Wrist warmers
Early 20th century
Made in the village of Graužai,
Viduklė District, Raseiniai County,
Lithuania
ŠAM EO 626/a, b

| **37.** |

Wrist warmers
Early 20th century
Made in Paežeris, Nemakščiai
District, Raseiniai County, Lithuania
ŠAM EO 622/a, b

| 38. |

Wrist warmers
Early 20th century
Made in Paežeris, Nemakščiai
District, Raseiniai County, Lithuania
ŠAM EO 629/a, b

| 39. |

Wrist warmer / *rankelka*
Early 20th century
Made in the village of Legotiškė,
Nemakščiai District, Raseiniai
County, Lithuania
ŠAM EO 623

| 40. |

Wrist warmers / *rankelkos*
Early 20th century
Made in the village of
Legotiškė, Nemakščiai
District, Raseiniai County,
Lithuania
ŠAM EO 627

| 41. |

Wrist warmers / *rankovėlės, rankelkos*
Second half of 20th century
Made in Mosėdis, in the region of Skuodas, Lithuania
ČDM E 4061/a, b

| 42. |

Wrist warmers / *rankovėlės, rankelkos*
Early 20th century
Made in Mosėdis, in the region of Skuodas, Lithuania
ČDM E 4062/a, b

| 44. |

Wrist warmers / *rankelkos, rankoviečiai*
Early 20th century
Made in the village of Juodainiai, Laukuva County, in the region of Šilalė, Lithuania
ŠAM EO 634/a, b

| 45. |

Wrist warmers
Late 19th or early 20th century
Made in the village of Kanteniai, Nevarėnai County, in the region of Telšiai, Lithuania
LDM LA 1552/a, b

| 43. |

Wrist warmer / *rankelka*
Early 20th century
Made in Šaukėnai, Kelmė region, Lithuania
ŠAM EO 630

| **46.** |

Wrist warmers / *rankelkos*
Early 20th century
Made in the village of Gilvyčiai,
Skaudvilė District, Tauragė County,
Lithuania
ŠAM EO 624/a, b

| **47.** |

Wrist warmers / *rankelkos*
Early 20th century
Made in the village of Gilvyčiai,
Skaudvilė District, Tauragė County,
Lithuania
ŠAM EO 640/a, b

| Klaipeda Region |

| 48. |

Wrist warmers / *maukos*
(moteriškos).
Made in Lankupiai, in the region
of Šilutė, Lithuania
LNM EMO 3041 /a, b

| Origin Unknown |

| **49.** |

Wrist warmers / *rankelka*
ŠAM EO 638

| **50.** |

Linen wrist warmer / *rankelka*
ŠAM EO 636

| **51.** |

Wrist warmers / *rankelka*
From a private donation.
ŠAM EO 3007

APPENDIX II:
LINEN AND COTTON FINGERLESS GLOVES

1.

Child's glove, early 20th century
From the village of Kniečiai,
Šimkaičiai District, Raseiniai
County, Lithuania
ČDME 4702

2.

Gloves with half fingers, early 20th century
From the village of Lelėnai,
Endrejavas County, in the region of Klaipėda, Lithuania
LDM LA 3420/a, b

| 3. |

Fingerless glove, early 20th century
From the village of Lelėnai, Endrejavas County, in the region of Klaipėda, Lithuania
LDM LD 161

| 4. |

Glove, early 20th century
From the village of Girkantiškė, Žarėnai County, in the region of Telšiai, Lithuania
LNM EMO 2140

| 5. |

Child's glove, early 20th century
From the village of Kniečiai, Šimkaičiai District, Raseiniai County, Lithuania
ČDME 4703

| 6. |

Wedding gloves, early 20th century
From Mažeikiai, Lithuania
MM GEK 3726/E1387

| 7. |

Fingerless gloves
Made in Kalvarija, Žemaičiai
County, in the region of Plungė,
Lithuania
ŽMA GEK 8182/a, b

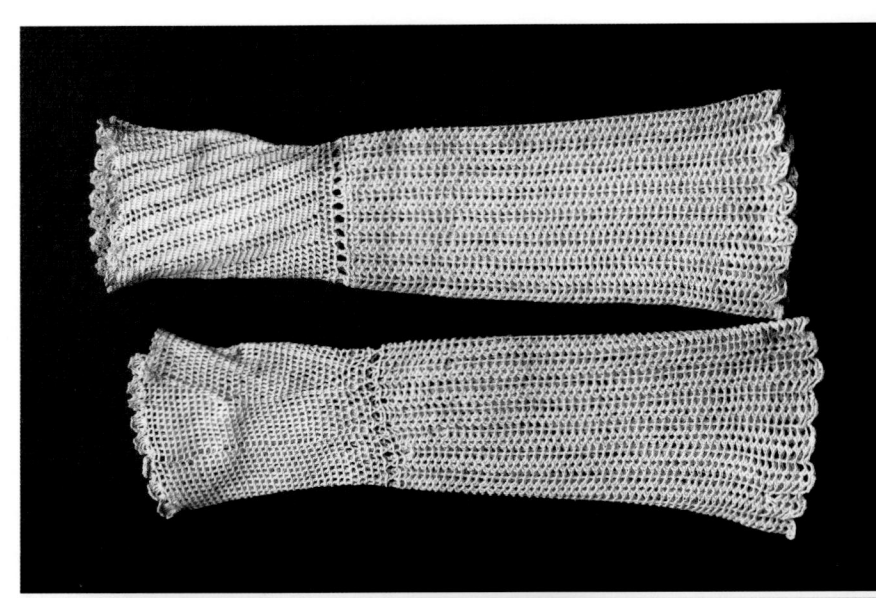

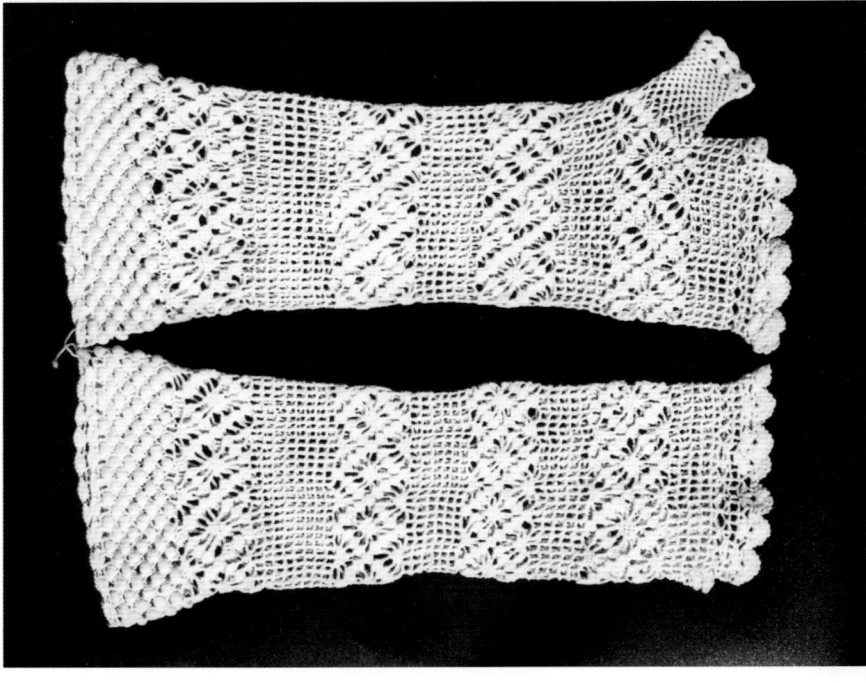

| **8.** |

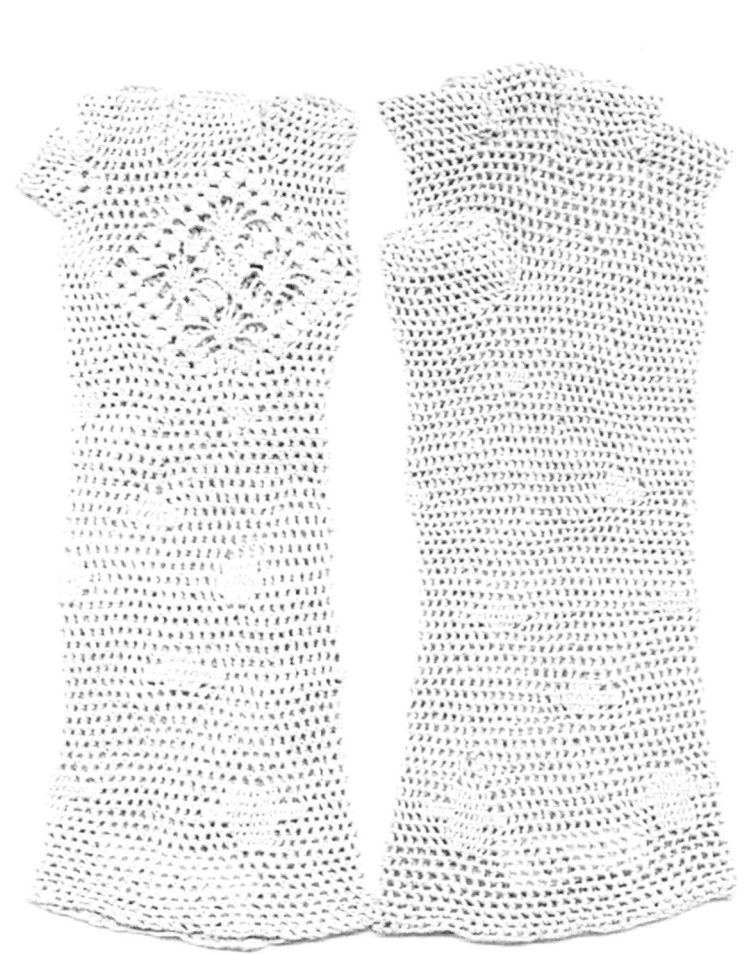

Women's gloves, early 20th century
From the village of Kegai, Žarėnai
County, in the region of Telšiai,
Lithuania
LDM LD 30/a, b

Contributors

1. Janina Birietienė, born in 1933 in the region of Anykščiai; living in Birzai since 1979.
2. Aldona Botinienė, born in 1958 in Panevėžys; living in Būtingė since 1982.
3. Marytė Čižienė, née Jankauskaitė, born in 1930 in the region of Molėtai, Skudutiškis County, in the village of Paalskse; living in in the region of Utena, Kuktiškių County, in the village of Bareišiai, since 1954.
4. Emilija Drumstienė, née Griganavičiūtė, born in 1942 in the village of Rliaius, Kavarskas County, in the region of Anykščiai; living in Klaipėda since 1976.
5. Ona Gimžauskienė, née Petravičiūtė, born in 1942 in the village of Gaideliai, Švenčionys County; currently living in the village of Kemešys, in the region of Utena.
6. Monika Kriukelienė, née Bareišytė, born in 1920 in the village of Pagrandžio, Rokiškis County; living in Vilnius since 1957.
7. Teofilė Kulakauskienė, née Laučytė, born in 1928 in the village of Butrimiškiai, Butrimoniai County, in the region of Alytus; currently living in Kaunas.
8. Vytautas Kunigėlis, born 1944 in the town of Kuktiškių, in the region of Utena; currently living in Vilnius.
9. Edita Meškuotienė, née Kuzavinytė, born in 1936 in Šeduva; living in Vilnius since 1958.
10. Albina Miglinienė, née Laučytė, born in 1924 in the village of Butrimiškiai, Butrimoniai County, in the region of Alytus; currently living in the village of Likiškių, in the same region.
11. Asta Miltenytė, born in 1959 in Ylakiai, in the region of Skuodas; currently living in Vilnius.
12. Mečislovas Algimantas Narušis, born in 1937 in Antanava, in the region of Molėtai; currently living in Vilkija.
13. Dormantė Penkinski, née Reškevičiūtė, born in 1957 and living in the village of Gojus in Rūdiškės Parish, in the region of Trakai.
14. Stasė Petraškienė, née Laučytė, born 1932 in the village of Butrimiškiai, Butrimoniai County, in the region of Alytus; now living in the village of Santaika, Santaikos District, in the same region.
15. Genovaitė Povilaitienė, née Jovaišaitė, born in 1949 in the town of Joniškis; currently living in Vilnius.
16. Elena Povilaitienė, née Krikščiūnaitė, born in 1943 in Panevėžys; currently living in Kaunas.
17. Palmyra Ragauskienė, née Baltušytė, born in 1931 in the village of Paškučiai, Papiliaus Parish, in the region of Biržai; currently living in Biržai.
18. Živilė Ramelienė, née Jurevičiūtė, born in 1950 in Vilnius and still living there.
19. Ritonė Šalkauskienė, née Tamulytė, born in 1943 in the village of Dapkūniškiai, Balninkai, in the region of Moletai; living in Vilnius since 1962.
20. Genovaitė Terlikovska, née Tijūnėlytė, born in 1946 in the village of Kretuonai, in the region of Švenčionys; currently living in Vilnius.
21. Antanina Trimonienė, née Jazgevičiūtė, born in 1922 in Siberia in the town of Biro, in the region of Khabarovsk; currently living in the village of Vijeikiai, Mockėnai County, in the region of Utena.
22. Ona Vileišienė, née Ažunarytė, born in 1917 in Mieleišiai; currently living in Biržai.

Stories from Contributors

1. Živilė Jurevičiūtė-Ramelienė (born in Vilnius in 1950) recounted her mother's memories. Rosalia Požélaite-Jurevičienė (1919-1995) was born in Linkuva, Pakruojis District. She later lived in Vilnius, but always considered herself a "Linkuvian." Her mother (Živilė's grandmother) Elena Pašakinskaitė-Požėlienė (1870- 1944, Pakruojis District) told her, "Both men and women wore wrist warmers every day, especially in the cold weather, while working in the fields and in the forests. At the time, shirts and blouses had wide sleeves, and wrist warmers were used to gather the sleeve in at the cuff so it would be warmer while working or driving horse-drawn carts. Everyday wrist warmers were knitted in stockinette stitch or ribbing. Some were monochrome but others were made in colorwork with diamonds, lattices, and other patterns. Holiday wrist warmers were decorated with glass beads. I didn't wear wrist warmers," Živilė's grandmother said. "The times changed—fashion changed." (Written by the author in 2002.)

2. Janina Birietienė (born in 1933 in the region of Anykščiai, and living in Birzai since 1979) described the following:

"My aunt Eleana Audickiene, who lived in Anykščiai, was born in the village of Mašinka in Troškūnai District. In 1908, she remembers people wearing wrist warmers when going to church or having celebrations with their neighbors. I was a child of about 6 years old, and I was very intrigued by the wrist warmers, because the beads would sparkle from under people's sleeves. Who knitted them, I don't know." (Written by Snieguolė Kubiliūtė in 2003.)

3. Around 1937 Ona Ažunarytė-Vileišienė (born in 1917 in Mieleišiai, and now living in Biržai) saw "beaded wrist warmers peeking out from under coat sleeves." She remembers that "around 1930-1934 in the village of Mieleišiai, Jozas Kuccinskas's sister, Joana

---

Stories are presented by date, in the order in which they were recorded.

Nemanienė, made him beaded wrist warmers." She also said, "Juozas was about 30 years old at that time." (Written by Snieguolė Kubiliūtė in 2003.)

4. Palmyra Baltušytė-Ragauskienė (born in 1931 in the village of Paškučiai, Papiliaus Parish, in the region of Biržai and now living in Biržai) remembers hearing that "wrist warmers without beads, called '*mankietais*,' were worn to keep warm." (Written by Snieguolė Kubiliūtė in 2003.)

5. Asta Miltenytė (born in 1959 in Ylakiai, in the region of Skuodas), wrote this story in 2005:

"My great-grandmother Marciana Varapnickaitė-Vasiliauskienė was from the village of Dilbikiai in Ylakiai District, in the region of Skuodas, and later moved to the village of Račaliai. I don't know when she was born, but she lived for a long time and died in 1935. Her daughter (my grandmother) Petronelė Vasiliauskaitė-Juzumienė (1878-1959) was born in the village of Račaliai, in Židikiai District, Mažeikiai County, and she moved to Šiliai, where in 1925 my mother, Emilija Juzumaitė-Miltenienė, was born. She remembered two pairs of wrist warmers: One pair was purple, and the other was burgundy with clear glass beads. They had always been in the house, but neither her mother nor her grandmother wore them. My mother assumed the wrist warmers had probably been knitted by her grandmother Marciana, because her mother Petronelle married early, gave birth to thirteen children, and did not have much time for such work. We have a lot of old family photos, but none of them show any women wearing wrist warmers. My mother didn't remember any men wearing wrist warmers. She was the youngest child, so that's probably why she never saw how the wrist warmers were made. My mother's older sister remembered seeing wrist warmers in their home.

"I once found a black pair of wrist warmers with white beads from Ylakiai, in the region of Skuodas. They were in the attic of Leokadija Vaitilavičienė's house, which we've rented since 1964 or 1965. I don't know when Leokadija was born, but it was around the turn of the century, and she was about the same age as my grandmother. I guess those black wrist warmers were hers. I also found another pair there, which were even nicer to me: black with pink and black sparkly beads. Of these, only the beads remain. I don't remember the pattern of wrist warmers because I was only a few years old. It wasn't a flower pattern; maybe it was more like a wavy band. No one called these *riešinės*. We used the Russian word, *rukavičnikais*."

6. Genovaitė Tienūnėlytė-Terlikovskaya was born in 1946 in the village of Kretuonai, in the region of Švenčionys; her grandmother, Kazimiera Rastenytė-Urbonienė, who was 84 years old when she died in 1967, wore wrist warmers. They were worn every day to keep warm, and were usually made from dark-colored wool yarn. Genovaitė's grandmother lived in the former Kurniskes palivark at Švenčionys County. (Recorded by Regina Jasaitytė-Šarkienė in 2006.)

7. Vytautas Kunigėlis was born in 1944 in the town of Kuktiškių, in the region of Utena, and currently lives in Vilnius; her mother, Kostancy Vrubliauskaitė-Kunigėlienė (1911-1991), also had wrist warmers. Konstancy was born in Riga, and in 1918 her parents returned to Lithuania, where she lived in the village of Kuktiškiai, Utena District, until her death. Vytautas remembers that when he was a child, he discovered mysterious items in a closet, knitted with beautiful patterns. They looked like long glove cuffs. His mother explained that they were wrist warmers. Vytautas was only about 6 or 7 years old at the time (around 1950-1951). Vytautas's mother mostly made crocheted tablecloths. Since her sister Bronė Vrubliauskaitė (1909-1993) knitted socks and gloves, it seems like she must also have made the wrist warmers. (Written by the author in 2006.)

8. Ona Petravičiūtė-Gimžauskienė (born in 1942 in the village of Gaideliai in the region of Švenčionys; currently living in the village of Kemešys, in the region of Utena) remembers seeing people wearing wrist warmers when she was about 5 or 6 years old:

"Elena Lašinskaitė, who lived in Kemešys until she died 44 years ago, wore knitted wrist warmers and leg warmers. She wore bare feet under galoshes, with the legwarmers above her ankles. They were about 8 inches (20 cm) long, and were usually made with linen yarns and worked in knit 2, purl 2 ribbing. I think she wore these for her health, because she had a skin disease (erysipelas)." (Written by the author in 2006.)

9. Elena Krikščiūnaitė-Povilaitienė (born in 1943 in Panevėžys; now living in Kaunas) remembers her mother Elena Padrigailaitė-Krikščiūnienė (1915-1992, born in Naugardė, in the region of Grodno, and living most of her life in Panevėžys) knitting wrist warmers. She said her mother did have a pair of beaded wrist warmers. (Written by Vida Belkytė-Snieckuvienė in 2006.)

10. Mecislovas Algimantas Narušis (born in 1937 in Antanava, in the region of Molėtai; currently living in Vilkija) remembers how his mother Monika Paškevičiūtė-Narušienė (born in 1896 in Antanava, in the region of Molėtai, in the area of Alanta; died at the age of 86) always wore something on her wrists to keep warm when she was in Siberian exile. These wrist warmers were made without beads, but they were knitted in beautiful patterns, or sometimes crocheted. (Written by Vida Belkytė-Snieckuvienė in 2006.)

11. Ritonės Tamulytė-Šalkauskienė was born in 1943 in the village of Dapkūniškiai, Balninkai County, in the region of Moletai, and has been living in Vilnius since 1962; in 1940, her mother, Apolonia Ylita-Tamulienė (1908-2004, born in Luciūnai, Kurkliai District, in the region of Anykščiai) went to Dapkūniškiai. She loved handwork very much; she did embroidery, knitting, and weaving. She made everything with handspun yarn, except for one pair of wrist warmers. These were knitted from purchased "*lučkai*" yarn, which was incredibly fine and soft. The wrist warmers were like braids, knitted in a diamond pattern with two colors of yarn: pale green and blue, like the depths of the sea. The main color was green. The wrist warmers could have been knitted by her mother, Ritonės's grandmother. Because no one wore the wrist warmers, her daughters later unraveled them and used the materials for embroidery. (Written by the author in 2008.)

12. Antanina Jazgevičiūtė-Trimonienė was born in 1922 in Siberia in the town of Biro, in the region of Khabarovsk. In 1925 her parents returned to Lithuania and settled in the village of Aliai, Mockėnai County, in the region of Utena. Today, Antanina lives in the village of Vijeikiai. She says:

"Verutė Vasiliauskaitė had wrist warmers made in bright colors: pink, red, yellow, maroon, orange, and blue. He wore them to walk to school. They were made in knit two, purl two ribbing by Verutė's mother, Vasiliauskienė-Jazgevičienė. How do I know that? Because Jazgevičius was my father's brother and married to a widow. It could have been around 1930 when I was in first grade at Utena r. Medeniai Elementary School in the village of Katlėriai. Verutė Vasiliauskaitė had come from the nearby village of Vyžuonos. The children were always asking Verutė to let them try on at least one wrist warmer. Verutė didn't want to, but he always ended up letting them anyway." (Written by author in 2008.)

13. "Marija Ruseckaitė-Reškevičienė, born in 1919 in Kaunas, had wrist warmers, or maybe she still has them. They were knitted in black yarn with a small pattern in various colors and were quite long," said her daughter, Dormantė Reškevičiūtė-Penkinski, born in 1957 and living in the village of Gojus in Rūdiškės Parish, in the region of Trakai. (Written by the author in 2008.)

14. Marytė Jankauskaitė-Čižienė was born in 1930 in in the region of Molėtai, Skudutiškis District, in the village of Paalsksė, and has been living since 1954 in the region of Utena, Kuktiškių County, in the village of Bareišiai. She was orphaned when she was very young, and began to knit when she was about 15 or 16 years old, after watching her friends. The friend who taught her, Bronė Štaraitė-Marcinkevičienė, from the same Paalskė district, was three years younger than she was. Bronė made up patterns, and then she taught them to her friends. The girls knitted socks, wrist warmers, and gloves, especially during the war years when there was no way to buy them. The wrist warmers were made with green, red, and black yarn that they dyed themselves, and worked in stockinette stitch with colorwork patterns of tulips and crosses. These decorative wrist warmers weren't to wear at home. They were only for going to church, dances, or markets. On the edge near the hand, these were decorated with little bobbles, and they had a cord to gather them in at the wrist. She may have had three pairs of wrist warmers. She usually wore them on bare arms with short sleeves, and they slid down to her hands. When they were worn with a long-sleeved blouse or dress, they would be worn over the cuffs. We called them *riešinės* because we wore them on our wrists. (Written by the author in 2008.)

15, 16, 17. Three sisters share their stories: Stasė Laučytė-Petraškienė (born in 1932 in the village of Butrimiškiai, Butrimoniai County, in the region of Alytus; currently living in the village of Santaika, Santaikos County, in the region of Alytus), Teofilė Laučytė-Kulakauskienė (born in 1928; currently living in Kaunas), and Albina Laučytė-Miglinienė (born in 1924; currently living in the village of Likiškių, in the region of Alytus).

Teofilė Kulakauskienė said:

"Old Man Senūta lived in the village of Panemunykas, in Rumboniai Parish. He had a sister, Katriutę Senuteitė, who was born before the 1863 uprising (the 'January Uprising' against the Russian Empire). She was a sweet little old lady who wouldn't hurt a fly, and she made wrist warmers. Katriutė loved my sister Albina very much, and gave her some wrist warmers."

Albina said: "I brought the wrist warmers home and they made me feel beautiful. I was so happy. She gave me two pairs: one had beads. The other pair was knitted in colorful yarn, but I don't have them anymore. When she was young, our father's mother, Pangonytė-Laučienė (born in Alytus District, 1863), wore wrist warmers, too."

Stasė: "She wore them under her coat, and you could see them under the sleeves."

Teofilė: "To church, to weddings. She also had a black hat with beads. When she died, she left them in her hope chest. She called them *rankafkas* ('hand warmers')."

Stasė: "Our mother didn't wear them because they were out of style. When I was young, she gave them to me. I unraveled them and used the beads on a black velvet dress. It was beautiful. I didn't use them for anything else. I do not know what they were called—maybe *rankogaliai* ('cuffs')." (Written by Dovilė Kulakauskienė, born in 1969 and currently living in Kaunas, in 2008.)

18. Aldona Botinienė (born in 1958 in Panevėžys) moved to Būtingė near the Latvian border when she got married in 1982. Her mother-in-law was Latvian and her father-in-law was Russian, so she learned about many different textile traditions. She inherited wrist warmers from Kotryna Brakšienė (née Ektė), who was born in 1924 and married into a Latvian family in Būtingė, and had lived in the house Aldona moved into. Her mother, Kotryna Ektienė, died in 1965. Kotryna Brakšienė, who died 4 years ago, wore wrist warmers with all kinds of jewelry such as brooches and pendants. Sometimes she showed them off to the family, and they enjoyed seeing the beautiful handcrafts. She was an excellent glove knitter, but she didn't really knit wrist warmers. Those had most likely been made by her grandmother, because her mother didn't do needlework. (Written by Zita Baniulaitytė in 2008.)

19. Monika Bareišytė-Kriukelienė (born in 1920 in in the village of Pagrandžio, Rokiškis County, and living in Vilnius since 1957), is well known in Lithuania for weaving and making folk costumes. She remembers that her grandmother Ona Zelenkauskienė (unknown date of birth, lived in the village of Pagrandžių, Rokiškis County, and died about 1932) knit and wore wrist warmers using special "*lučkai*" yarn in gradient colors. She said that whenever her grandmother wore her coat to go out, she also wore wrist warmers to keep her wrists warm. The wrist warmers were very colorful, beautiful and comfortable, knitted in garter stitch. When their grandmother wasn't looking, both of Monika's sisters would try on wrist warmers, even putting both hands into one. Whenever their grandmother caught them doing this, she scolded them, saying, "You'll stretch the wrist warmers out of shape." (Written by the author in 2008.)

20. Zemgale Genovaitė Jovaišaitė-Povilaitienė (born in 1949 in the town of Joniškis) says:

"My mother, Genovaitė Indriulytė-Jovaišienė (1922-1978, born in Joniškis), loved doing handicrafts. After returning from exile in Siberia, she'd missed doing handicrafts so much that when she was raising her children, she would stay up late at night to knit and do embroidery. Our whole house was decorated with my mother's embroidery work. Like all of the women in our family, my mother made beautiful socks, gloves, and wrist warmers. She would travel to Riga to go to the market to buy yarn, dyes, and other supplies. That's where she bought beads, too. Her favorite color was burgundy. The wrist warmers were knitted in garter stitch, with a main color and stripes made from scraps of contrasting colors of yarn. These also were decorated with a beaded zigzag pattern. I remember well my mother's beaded wrist warmers—burgundy yarn with a white beaded pattern going up and down, up and down, in wide and narrow stripes. We had a lot of wrist warmers. My mother knit them for herself, for me, and for my sister and brother. Only my father, for some reason, didn't wear them.

"I've been wearing wrist warmers since I was 11 or 12, going to class and doing after-school activities with my friends. When the cold weather arrives, wrist warmers are indispensable. We wore them under our sleeve cuffs. When the wrist warmers were new, we would pull up our sleeves so everyone could see them. I had a beautiful red wool dress, and the sleeves barely covered the wrist warmers (perhaps I was outgrowing it). I felt like I was dressing up whenever I wore them. These wrist warmers were about 3½ or 4 inches (8-10 cm) long. At 11 or 12 years old, we were still such children—the wrist warmers were all we needed to be dressed up; we never even thought about wearing makeup. I don't remember if we had a special name for them.

"My uncles also wore wrist warmers. Their sister, my mother, made them plain wrist warmers in burgundy or black. Men also wore beautiful wrist warmers under their white shirt cuffs. The wrist warmers did not have another name, so they called them *riešinės*. I did not wear warmers when I went to college—it's a village tradition, not a fashion."

Around 1965-1969, Genovaitė Povilaitienė studied at the conservatory. The compulsory singing was taught by a former opera singer, Professor Petras Oleka. He had a variety of wrist warmers, both plain and with patterns, to go with different clothes. The most interesting thing about the professor's wrist warmers is that they were attached to the little finger with a crochet loop. (Written by the author in 2008.)

21. Emilija Griganavičiūtė-Drumstienė (born in 1942 in the village of Rliaius, Kavarskas County, in the region of Anykščiai, and living in Klaipėda since 1976) knitted wrist warmers in knit and purl ribbing with white or gray wool—always natural, undyed colors. They were about as long as the distance between her thumb and her little finger spread out as far as they could go. As soon as the weather cooled down, she broke out her wrist warmers. She also knitted knee warmers. Emilija is convinced that her wrist warmers helped her avoid joint pain. (Written by the author in 2008.)

22. Edita Kuzavinytė-Meškuotienė (born in 1936 in Šeduva) remembers from her mother's stories that her mother's grandmother wore wrist warmers. Edita's great grandmother, Agota Smalinskienė (lived around 1840-1912, Obeliai District) always wanted her wrists to be warm, and she even wore her wrist warmers indoors. Edita's mother, Emilija Zaukaitė-Kuzavinienė (1903-1992) wore her wrist warmers when she wore the Lithuanian national costume to keep her hands warm. They just covered her cuffs. She wore her wrist warmers everywhere she went—to church, to visit friends. These wrist warmers were knitted in garter stitch stripes using two colors. They were made without beads, because they couldn't afford any. (Written by the author in 2008.)

Sources

I. Wrist warmers from these museum collections are featured:
   1. Birzai Sėla Museum
   2. Kaisiadorys Museum
   3. Lithuanian Art Museum
   4. Open-Air Museum of Lithuania
   5. Lithuanian National Museum
   6. Marijampolė Regional Museum)
   7. Mažeikiai Museum
   8. M. K. Čiurlionis National Museum of Art
   9. Palanga Traditional Textile Training Center
   10. Panevėžys Regional Museum
   11. Šiauliai Aušra museum
   12. Antanas and Anastasias Tamošaičiai Gallery "Židinys"
   13. Upyna Folk Art Museum (Šilalė county)
   14. Vilkaviškis Regional Museum
   15. Samogitian Alka Museum

II. Wrist warmers from these publications are featured.
   1. M. Glemžaitė. *Lietuvių tautiniai drabužiai*. Vilnius. 1955, 55 psl.
   2. Irena Regina Merkienė. Marija Pautieniūtė–Banionienė. *Lietuvininkų pirštinės* // Lietuvos etnologija. 3, Vilnius: Žara. 1998, 191 psl.
   3. LNM archyvas. Byla Nr. 62, 22 psl.

III. Wrist warmers from the personal collections of Lucija Dobrickienė, Dovilė Kulakauskienė, Astė Miltenytė, Raimonda Narbutienė and Živilė Jurevičiūtė-Ramelienė are featured.

IV. Patterns adapted from other accessories, such as a dicky embellished with beads in the M. K. Čiurlionis National Museum of Art collection, are also featured.

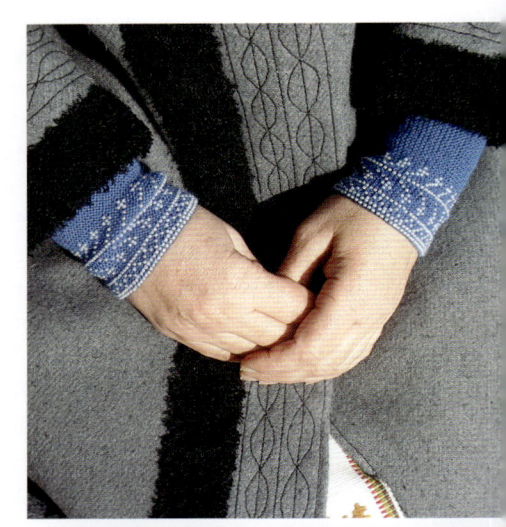

References

1. Aleknienė O. D. *Riešinės–iš užmaršties prikeltos miniatiūros* // Liaudies kultūra. No. 6, 2007, pgs. 68–72.
2. Bernotaitė-Beliauskienė D. *Žemaičių moterų drabužiai XIX–XX a. pradžioje* // Šeimininkė. Sept. 11, 2002. No. 37(547).
3. Bernotienė S. *Lietuvių liaudies moterų drabužiai XVIII a. pab.–XX a. pr.*, Vilnius: Mintis, 1974.
4. Druchunas, Donna. *Arctic Lace. Knitting Projects and Stories Inspired by Alaska's Native Knitters.* // Nomad press. Fort Collins, Colorado, 2006, pg. 122.
5. Jurkuvienė T. *Lietuvių tautinis kostiumas* // Vilnius: Baltos lankos, 2006.
6. Jurkuvienė T. *Pagalbiniai reikmenys* // Liaudies kultūra. No. 3, 1993, pages 46–47.
7. Juškienė I. F. *Riešinės* // Vilnius: UAB "Petro ofsetas," 2005.
8. Gaigalienė L. *XVI – XIX a. Siuviniai. Katalogas* // LTSR Istorijos ir etnografijos muziejaus leidinys. Vilnius. 1988.
9. Glemžaitė M. *Lietuvių tautiniai drabužiai*. Vilnius: Valstybinė politinės ir mokslinės literatūros leidykla, 1955.
10. Kuncienė O. *IX–XIII a. stiklo karoliai Lietuvoje* // Lietuvos archeologija. No. 2, 1981, pgs. 77–90.
11. *Lietuvių tautiniai rūbai.* Vilnius: Scena. 1994.
12. Lietuvių liaudies menas: *Drabužiai* // Sudarė J. Balčikonis, S. Bernotienė, K. Kairiūkštytė-Galaunienė, A. Mikėnaitė. Vilnius: Vaga,1974.
13. Merkienė I. R., Pautieniūtė-Banionienė M. *Lietuvininkų pirštinės* // Lietuvos etnologija. No. 3, Vilnius: Žara. 1998.
14. Rasmussen Noble, Carol. *Knitting Fair Isle Mittens & Gloves: 40 Great-Looking Designs.* // Lark Books, Asheville, North Carolina, 2002, page 11.
15. *Perler på pulsen*. Kirsten Rømcke, Nina Granlund Sæther // Norges Hus idslag. 2004.
16. Piskorz–Branekova E. *Polskie stroje ludowe* // Sport I turystyka – Muza Sa. // Warszawa. 2005, pgs. 36–41.
17. Sikorskienė V. *Riešinės* // Rankdarbiai plius visažinis. No. 129, December, 2001.
18. Tamošaitis A. *Lietuvių moterų tautiniai drabužiai* // Sodžiaus menas. Kaunas: Žemės Ūkio Rūmų leidykla. 1939.
19. Гендертон Люсинда. *Бисер. Большая иллюстрированная энциклопедия.* // Москва: Эксмо. 2007.

| Abbreviations |

BKM–*Biržų krašto muziejus "Sėla"* (Birzai Sėla Museum)
ČDM–*Nacionalinis M. K. Čiurlionio dailės muziejus* (M. K. Čiurlionis National Museum of Art)
E–*Nacionalinio M. K. Čiurlionio dailės muziejaus* (M. K. Čiurlionis National Museum of Art) exhibit inventory call number
EMO–*Lietuvos nacionalinio muziejaus* (Lithuanian National Museum) exhibit inventory call number
EO – *Šiaulių "Aušros" muziejaus* (Siauliai Aušra Museum) exhibit inventory call number
GEK – Museum catalog numbers from the Birzai Sėla Museum, Marijampolė Regional Museum, Panevėžys Regional Museum, Vilkaviškis Regional Museum, and the Samogitian Alka Museum
LA, LD, LS – *Lietuvos dailės muziejaus* (Lithuanian Art Museum) exhibit inventory call number
LBM–*Lietuvos liaudies buities muziejus* (Open-Air Museum of Lithuania)
LDM–*Lietuvos dailės muziejus* (Lithuanian Art Museum)
LNM–*Lietuvos nacionalinis muziejus* (Lithuanian National Museum)
MKM–*Marijampolės kraštotyros muziejus* (Marijampolė Regional Museum)
MM – *Mažeikių muziejus* (Mažeikiai Museum)
PKM – *Panevėžio kraštotyros muziejus* (Panevėžys Regional Museum)
ŠAM – *Šiaulių "Aušros" muziejus* (Siauliai Aušra Museum)
VKM – *Vilkaviškio krašto muziejus* (Vilkaviškis Regional Museum)
ŽMA – *Žemaičių muziejus "Alka"* (Samogitian "Alka" Museum)

| Knitting Abbreviations |

BO—bind off
CO—cast on
k—knit
p—purl
RS—right side
st(s)—stitch(es)
WS—wrong side

| List of Wrist Warmers Organized by Ethnographic Region |

| Wrist Warmers from Aukštaitija |

A. With Beads

1. Wrist warmers
Made in Biržai County, Lithuania
2¾ x 3¼ in / 7 x 8 cm
BKM GEK 825[21]
Project Illustrations 1 and 2[22]

2. Wrist warmers
Made in the village of Deikiškiai, Vabalninkas County, in the region of Biržai, Lithuania
3¼ x 3¼ in / 8 x 8 cm
BKM GEK 3557
Project Illustrations 3 and 4

3. Men's wrist warmers / *rankovėlės*[23]
Late 19th century
3½ x 3½ in / 9 x 9 cm
Made in Pabiržė District, Biržai County, Lithuania
ČDM E 1547/a, b
Project Illustrations 5 and 6

4. Wrist warmers / *rankovėlės*
19th century
3½ x 3¼ in / 9 x 8 cm
Made in the village of Užugulbinė, Pabiržė District, Biržai County, Lithuania
ČDM E 1549/a, b
Project Illustrations 7 and 8

5. Glove
Made in the village of Užugulbinė, Pabiržė District, Biržai County, Lithuania
ČDM E 1573
Project Illustrations 9 and 10

6. Wrist warmers / *rankovėlės*
19th century
Made in the village of Rinkuškiai, Biržai District, Biržai County, Lithuania
3¾ x 3 in / 9.5 x 7.5 cm
ČDM E 1575/a, b
Project Illustrations 11 and 12

7. Embellished wrist warmers / *rankovėlės*
Early 20th century
Knit by O. D. Aleknienė.
Made in the village of Rinkuškiai, Biržai District, Biržai County, Lithuania
3¾ x 7¾ in / 9.5 x 19.5 cm (stretched out)
ČDM E 1550/a, b
Project Illustrations 13 and 14

8. Men's wrist warmers / *runkauka*
Late 19th century
From the farmstead of Kvietkeliai, Biržai County, Lithuania
4¾ x 4½ in / 12 x 11.5 cm
LNM EMO1601
Project Illustrations 15 and 16

9. Wrist warmers / *rankovėlės*
Made in Biržai County, Lithuania
5½ x 4 in / 14 x 10 cm
ČDM E 1546/a, b
Project Illustrations 17 and 18

10. Wrist warmers / *rankovėlės*
Made in the village of Pilsupiai, Josvainiai District, Kėdainiai, Lithuania
6 x 3¼ in / 15 x 8.5 cm
ČDM E 1567/a, b
Project Illustrations 19 and 20

11. Dicky
Late 19th century
Made in Pasvalis County, Lithuania
Bead pattern adapted for wrist warmers
ČDM E 3869
Project Illustrations 21 and 22

12. Wrist warmers
Early 20th century
Made in Linkuva, in the region of Pakruojis, Lithuania
2½ x 2¾ in / 6.5 x 7 cm
From Živilė Jurevičiūtė-Ramelienė's personal collection
Project Illustrations 23 and 24

13. Wrist warmers / *rankaukos*
19th century
From the village of Liūneliai, Vidiškiai County, in the region of Ukmergė, Lithuania
3½ x 3¼ in / 9 x 8.5 cm
LDM LA 2318/a,b
Project Illustrations 25 and 26

14. Wrist warmers / *rankauka*
Early 20th century
Made in the village of Rudikuai, Kupiškis District, Panevėžys County, Lithuania
3¾ x 3½ in / 9.8 x 9 cm
ŠAM EO 467
Project Illustrations 27 and 28

15. Wrist warmers
19th century
Made in the village of Varniškis, Antašava County, in the region of Kupiškis, Lithuania
3½ x 3¼ in / 9 x 8.5 cm
LDM LA 1466/a,b
Project Illustrations 29 and 30

16. Wrist warmers / *rukavicos*
Late 19th century
Made in the village of Laibgaliai, Rokiškis District, Rokiškis County, Lithuania
3½ x 3¼ in / 9 x 8 cm
LNM EMO 6339/a,b
Project Illustrations 31 and 32

17. Wrist warmer / *rankovėlė*
Late 19th century
Made in the village of Liepiškiai, Šiaulėnai District, Šiauliai County, Lithuania
4¼ x 3½ in / 10.5 x 9 cm
ČDM E 1566
Project Illustrations 33 and 34

18.
Wrist warmer
Made in Rumšiškis County, in the region of Kaunas, Lithuania

---

[21] Information is listed as specified in museum archives. The names of villages and municipalities have been changed to match the list of standardized residential names in Lietuvos TSR administracinio-teritorinio suskirstymo "žinyno" D. 2 2nd edition. (Vilnius in 1976)
[22] Project Illustrations refer to the patterns and charts on pages 22–128. The original wrist warmers are shown on the right-hand page, with the knitting chart and details on the left.
[23] The second word listed is the name for wrist warmers used in the local dialect as recorded in museum records.

4¼ x 3½ in / 10.5 x 9 cm
LNM EMO 1856
Project Illustrations 35 and 36

B. Without Beads

19. Wrist warmers / *rankovėlės*
Late 19th century
Made in the town of Pabiržė, Biržai County, Lithuania
4½ x 3¼ in / 11.5 x 8.5 cm
ČDM E 1541/a, b
Figure 1, page 150

20. Wrist Warmers / *rankovėlės*
Late 19th or early 20th century
Made in the village of Latveliai, Nemunėlio Radviliškis District, in the region of Biržai, Lithuania
5 x 4½ in / 12.5 x 11.5 cm
ČDM E 1540/a, b
Figure 2, page 150

21. Wrist warmers / *rankovėlės*
Late 19th or early 20th century
Made in Pasvalys, Biržai County, Lithuania
4½ x 3½ in / 11.5 x 9 cm
ČDM E 1542 /a, b
Figure 3, page 151

22. Glove
Early 20th century
From the village of Liepiškiai, Šiaulėnai District, Šiauliai County, Lithuania
10½ in long x 4¼ in wide / 27 cm long x 11 cm wide
ČDM E 1557
Figure 4, page 151

23. Wrist warmers / *rankovėlės*
Late 19th or early 20th century
Made in Pasvalys, Biržai County, Lithuania
1¾ x 3¼ in / 4.5 x 8 cm
ČDM E 1548/a, b
Figure 5, page 151

| Wrist Warmers from Dzūkija |

A. With Beads

1. Wrist warmers
Late 19th century
Made in the village of Geruliai, Balbieriškis County, in the region of Prienai, Lithuania
4¼ x 3½ in / 10.5 x 9 cm
LDM LA 1946/a,b
Project Illustrations 37 and 38

2. Wrist warmers / *rankapkos*
Late 19th century
Made in the village of Norkūnai, Balbieriškis County, in the region of Prienai, Lithuania
3½ x 3 in / 8.5 x 7.5 cm
LNM EMO 3892/a,b
Project Illustrations 39 and 40

3. Wrist warmers / *rankapkos*
Late 19th century
Made in the village of Norkūnai, Balbieriškis County, in the region of Prienai, Lithuania
2¾ x 3½ in / 7 x 8.5 cm
LNM EMO 3891/a,b
Project Illustrations 41 and 42

4. Wrist warmers / *rankovėlės*
Early 20th century
Made in the village of Naudžiūnai, Birštonas County, in the region of Prienai, Lithuania
4¼ x 3¼ in / 11 x 8 cm
ČDM E 5889/a,b
Project Illustrations 43 and 44

5. Wrist warmers
Made in Nemajūnai County, in the region of Jieznas, Lithuania
5¼ x 3½ in / 13.5 x 9 cm
LDM LD 163
Project Illustrations 45 and 46

6. Wrist warmer / *rankovėlė*
Early 20th century
Made in the village of Akmeniai, Kučiūnai County, in the region of Lazdijai, Lithuania
3½ x 3½ in / 9 x 9 cm
ČDM E 5573
Project Illustrations 47 and 48

7. Wrist warmers / *rankankos*
Made in the village of Panarvė, Šventežeris County, in the region of Lazdijai, Lithuania
3¼ x 3½ in / 8 x 9 cm
LBM 3696/567/a,b
Project Illustrations 49 and 50

8. Wrist warmers
19th century
Made in the village of Buteliūnai, Avižonys County, in the region of Veisiejai, Lithuania
a) 4¼ x 3½ in / 11 x 9 cm, b) 4¾ x 3½ in / 12 x 9 cm
LDM LA 24/a,b
Project Illustrations 51 and 52

9. Wrist warmers / *rankaukos*
Early 20th century
Made in the village of Krokininkai, Krokialaukis County, in the region of Alytus, Lithuania
4 x 3¼ in / 10 x 8 cm
LNM EMO 2345/a,b
Project Illustrations 53 and 54

10. Wrist warmers / *rankafkos*
Late 19th century
Made in the village of Panemunykai, Rumbonys Parish, Alytus County, Lithuania
4 x 3¼ in / 10 x 8.5 cm
From the private collection of Dovilė Kulakauskienė
Project Illustrations 55 and 56

11. Wrist warmers / *rankovėlės*
Early 20th Century
Made in the village of Kalviškiai, Seinai County (now Sejny, Poland)
4¼ x 3½ in / 11 x 9 cm
ČDM E 3870/a,b
Project Illustrations 57 and 58

12. Wrist warmers
Made in the village of Čižiūnai, in the area of Valkininkai, Trakai County, Lithuania
LNM archives, volume 62, page 22
Pattern reproduced by O. D. Aleknienė
Project Illustrations 59 and 60

13. Wrist warmers
19th century
Made in the village of Toliškės, Vilūnai County, in the region of Kaišiadorys, Lithuania
4¼ x 3½ in / 11 x 9 cm
LDM LA 5238/a,b
Project Illustrations 61 and 62

14. Wrist warmers / *rankaukos*
Late 19th or early 20th century
Made in the village of Užupiai, in the region of Kaišiadorys, Lithuania
4 x 3¼ in / 10 x 8 cm
LNM EMO 1855/a,b
Project Illustrations 63 and 64

15. Wrist warmers
Late 19th or early 20th century
Knit in ribbing with bead embroidery
Made in Druskininkai, Lithuania
3¼ x 3¼ in / 8.4 x 8 cm
LBM P-206/a, b
Figure 15, page 155

B. Without Beads

16. Wrist warmer
Late 19th or early 20th century
Made in the village of Kančėnai, Daugai County, in the region of Alytus, Lithuania
3½ x 3½ in / 9 x 9 cm

LDM LA 1123
Figure 6, page 152

17. Wrist warmer / *rankauka*
From the town of Meteliai, Seirijai District, Alytus County, Lithuania
3½ x 3½ in / 9 x 9 cm
ŠAM EO 625
Figure 7, page 152

18. Wrist warmers / *rankogaliai*, "zarankavkos"
Made in the village of Cigoniškiai, Parečėnų County, in the region of Alytus, Lithuania
4½ x 3 in / 11.5 x 7.5 cm
LBM 3712/568/a, b
Figure 8, page 152

19. Wrist warmers/knitted cuffs
From the village of Miežoniai, Palomenės County, in the region of Kaišiadorys, Lithuania
Made by Marijona Tomkutė-Balnienė (1883-1963). Donated by her granddaughter, Danutė Regina Katkevičienė (born 1936) living in Kaišiadorys, 2006
6¾ x 3¼ in / 16 x 8 cm
From the Kaišiadorys Museum collection
Figure 9, page 153

20. Wrist warmers / *runkaukos*
Made in the village of Avižieniai, Šlavantai County, in the region of Lazdijai, Lithuania
Hand: 4½ x 3¼ in / 11.5 x 8.5 cm / Wrist: 3 in / 7.5 cm
LNM EMO 5559/a, b
Figure 10, page 153

21. Wrist warmer / *rankauka*
Made in the village of Čižiūnai, Aukštadvaris District, Trakai County, Lithuania
Anastazija and Antanas Tamošaičiai Gallery "Židinys". Exhibit no. 230
3 x 3¼ in / 7.5 x 8 cm
Figure 11, page 153

22. Wrist warmers / *rankovėlės*, *rankaukos*
Early 20th century
Made in the village of Kristapiškiai, Lelioniai County, in the region of Prienai, Lithuania
5½ in / 14 cm long
ČDM E 3397/a, b
Figure 12, page 154

23. Wrist warmer / *rankauka*
Early 20th century
Made in the village of Kružiūnai, Balbieriškis County, in the region of Prienai, Lithuania
3½ x 3¼ in / 9 x 8 cm
LNM EMO 3893
Figure 13, page 154

24. Wrist warmers / *rankaukos*
20th century
Made in the village of Kunigiškiai, Balbieriškis County, in the region of Prienai, Lithuania
4¾ x 3½ in / 12 x 9 cm
LDM LA 4107/a, b
Figure 14, page 154

| Wrist Warmers from Suvalkija |

A. With Beads

1. Wrist warmers / *rankaukos*
Late 19th century
Made in the village of Mokolai, in the region of Marijampolė, Lithuania
a) 3¼ x 3¼ in / 8 x 8 cm, b) 3¼ x 3¼ in / 8 x 7.8cm
MKM GEK 981/a,b
Project Illustrations 65 and 66

2. Wrist warmers / *rankovėlės*
Made in Marijampolė, Lithuania
5 x 3½ in / 13 x 9 cm
ČDM E 1578/a,b
Project Illustrations 67 and 68

3. Wrist warmers
Late 19th century
Made in the village of Paprūdžiai, Pilviškiai County, in the region of Vilkaviškis, Lithuania
4¼ x 3 in / 11 x 7.5 cm
VKM GEK 1594/a,b
Project Illustrations 69 and 70

4. Wrist warmers / *rankovėlės*
Late 19th century
Made in Vilkaviškis, Lithuania
4¼ x 3½ in / 10.5 x 9 cm
ČDM E 1545/a,b
Project Illustrations 71 and 72

5. Wrist warmers / *rankaukos*
Early 20th century
Made in Gižai District, Vilkaviškis County, Lithuania
3¼ x 3¼ in / 8.5 x 8 cm
LNM EMO 4711/a,b
Project Illustrations 73 and 74

B. Without Beads

6. Wrist warmers
Late 19th century
Made in the village of Tarpučiai, Šunskai County, in the region of Marijampolė, Lithuania
4¼ x 3½ in / 10.5 x 9 cm
MKM GEK Nr.982/a, b
Figure 16, page 156

7. Wrist warmers
Early 20th century
Made in the village of Trakiškiai, Trakiškiai County, in the region of Marijampolė, Lithuania
4½ x 3½ in / 11.5 x 9 cm
MKM GEK 983/a, b
Figure 17, page 157

8. Wrist warmers
Early 20th century
Made in the village of Trakiškiai, Trakiškiai County, in the region of Marijampolė, Lithuania
5 x 4 in / 12.5 x 10 cm

MKM GEK Nr.984/a, b
Figure 18, page 157

9. Wrist warmers / *rankaukos*
Early 20th century
Made in Šunskai, Šunskai County, in the region of Marijampolė, Lithuania
4¼ x 3½ in / 11 x 9 cm
LDM LA 2190/a, b
Figure 19, page 157

10. Wrist warmers / *rankaukos*
Late 19th century
Made in Šunskai, Šunskai County, in the region of Marijampolė, Lithuania
5 x 3¼ in / 13 x 8 cm
LDM LA 2191/a, b
Figure 20, page 158

11. Wrist warmers / *rankaukos*
Second half of 19th century
Made in the village of Daukšiai, Padovinis County, in the region of Marijampolė, Lithuania
3½ x 3½ in / 9 x 9 cm; 4¼ x 3½ in / 11 x 9 cm
LDM LA 2207/a, b
Figure 21, page 158

12. Wrist warmers / *rankaukos*
Late 19th to early 20th century
Made in the village of Turlojiškė, Naujiena County, in the region of Marijampolė, Lithuania
4¼ x 4¼ in / 11 x 10.5 cm
LDM LA 2935 /a, b
Figure 22, page 158

13. Wrist warmer / *rankauka*
Late 19th to early 20th century
Made in the region of Marijampolė, Lithuania
4¼ x 3¾ in / 10.5 x 9.5 cm
LNM EMO 7383
Figure 23, page 159

14. Wrist warmer
Late 19th to early 20th century
Made in the village of Viliušiai,

Jankai County, in the region of Šakių, Lithuania
3¼ x 3½ in / 8 x 9 cm
LNM EMO 5558
Figure 24, page 159

15. Wrist warmer / *rankovėlė*
Made in Šakiai County, Lithuania
5½ in / 14 cm long
ČDM E 2410/a, b
Figure 25, page 160

16. Wrist warmer
Made in the village of Varčiuliai, Kiduliai District, Šakiai County, Lithuania
5¼ x 2¾ in / 13.5 x 7 cm
Anastazija and Antanas Tamošaičiai Gallery "Židinys." Exibit no. 231.
Figure 26, page 160

17. Wrist warmers / *rankaukos*
Made in Pilviškiai, Pilviškiai County, in the region of Vilkaviškis, Lithuania
4 x 3¾ in / 10 x 9.5 cm
LNM EMO 7467/a, b
Figure 27, page 160

18. Wrist warmers
Late 19th or early 20th century
Made in Suvalkija, Lithuania
Hand: 4¼ x 3¼ in / 10.5 x 8.5 cm; Wrist: 2¼ in / 6 cm
LNM EMO 9082/a, b
Figure 28, page 161

Wrist Warmers from Žemaitija

A. With Beads

1. Wrist warmers
Made in the village of Šventoji, in the region of Kretinga, Lithuania
5¼ x 7½ in / 13.5 x 19 cm (wrist circumference)
LDM LA 2168/a,b
Project Illustrations 75 and 76

2. Wrist warmers
Late 19th century
Made in Būtingė, Lithuania
3½ x 5 in / 9 x 13 cm
Palanga Traditional Textiles Education Center
Project Illustrations 77 and 78

3. Wrist warmers / *rankaukos*
Made in the village of Maigai, Mažeikiai District, Mažeikiai County, Lithuania
4 x 3¼ in / 10 x 8.5cm
LDM LA 4261/a,b
Project Illustrations 79 and 80

4. Wrist warmers
Made in the village of Užlieknė, Tirkšliai District, Mažeikiai County, Lithuania
3¼ x 3½ in / 8.5 x 9 cm
LDM LA 4685/a,b
Project Illustrations 81 and 82

5. Wrist warmers
Late 19th or early 20th century
Made in the area of Mažeikiai, Lithuania
3¼ x 4 in / 8.5 x 10 cm
MM E 1480/259
Project Illustrations 83 and 84

6. Wrist warmers
19th century
Made in the village of Latakai, Viduklė District, Raseiniai County, Lithuania
4 x 3½ in / 10 x 9 cm
ŠAM EO 455/a,b
Project Illustrations 85 and 86

7. Wrist warmers / *rankelkos*
19th century
Made in the village of Latakai, Viduklė District, Raseiniai County, Lithuania
4¼ x 3¼ in / 11 x 8 cm
ŠAM EO 456/a,b
Project Illustrations 87 and 88

8. Wrist warmer
Made in Rietavas, in the region of Plungė, Lithuania
4 x 3¼ in / 10 x 8 cm
LDM LA 4479
Project Illustrations 89 and 90

9. Wrist warmers / *mankietai*
Early 20th century
Made in the village of Meškiai, Šiaudinė County, in the region of Akmenė, Lithuania
3¼ in x 3¼ in / 8.5 x 8 cm
LDM LA 1353/a,b
Project Illustrations 91 and 92

10. Wrist warmers / *rankelkos*
Late 19th century
Made in Pagramantis, in the region of Tauragė, Lithuania
3¾ x 3¼ in / 9.5 x 8 cm
LNM EMO 1883/a,b
Project Illustrations 93 and 94

11. Wrist warmers / *rankelkos*
Early 20th century
Made in the village of Vaitimėnai, Mažonai County, in the region of Tauragė, Lithuania
3¾ x 3¼ in / 9.5 x 8.5 cm
Upyna Folk Art Museum (Šilalė county)
Exhibit nos. 1061 and 1062
Project Illustrations 95 and 96

12. Men's wrist warmers
Made in the region of Kelmė, Lithuania
4½ x 3½ in / 11.5 x 9 cm
LNM EMO 4251/a,b
Project Illustrations 97 and 98

13. Men's wrist warmers / *rankovėčiai*
Late 19th century
Made in the village of Kumžaičiai, Kuliai County, in the region of Plungė, Lithuania
3¾ x 3½ in / 9.5 x 9 cm
LNM EMO 2347/a,b
Project Illustrations 99 and 100

14. Wrist warmers / *rankelkos*
19th century
Made in Ylakiai, in the region of Skuodo, Lithuania
a) 3¼ x 3¼ in / 8.5 x 8.5 cm, b) 3½ x 3½ in / 9 x 9 cm
LDM LD 767/a,b
Project Illustrations 101 and 102

15. Wrist warmers / *rukavičnikai*
Early 20th century
Made in the village of Dilbikiai, Ylakiai County, in the region of Skuodo, Lithuania
3½ x 3¼ in / 9 x 8.2 cm
From the private collection of Asta Miltenytė
Project Illustrations 103 and 104

16. Wrist warmers / *rukavičnikai*
Early 20th century
Made in Ylakiai, in the region of Skuodo, Lithuania
5 x 3¾ in / 12.5 x 9.5 cm
From the private collection of Asta Miltenytė
Project Illustrations 105 and 106

17. Wrist warmers / *rankelkos*
Made in the village of Papaukštkalnis, Upyna County, in the region of Šilalė, Lithuania
3½ x 3¼ in / 9 x 8.5 cm
LNM EMO 8600/a,b
Project Illustrations 107 and 108

18. Wrist warmers / *rankelkos*
Early 20th century
Made in the village of Lingiai, Upyna County, in the region of Šilalė, Lithuania
3¼ x 3¼ in / 8 x 8 cm
Upyna Folk Art Museum (Šilalė county)
Exhibit nos. 2225 and 2226
Project Illustrations 109 and 110

19. Wrist warmers
Made in Tryškiai, in the region of Telšiai, Lithuania.
3¼ x 3¼ in / 8 x 8 cm
LDM LS 274/a,b
Project Illustrations 111 and 112

20. Wrist warmers
Made in Tryškiai, in the region of Telšiai, Lithuania
3¼ x 3¼ in / 8 x 8 cm
LDM LS 275/a,b
Project Illustrations 113 and 114

B. Without Beads

21. Wrist warmers / *rankogaliai*
Early 20th century
Made in Viekšniai, in the region of Akmenė, Lithuania
MM GEK 1479 E 258/a, b
Figure 29, page 162

22. Women's wrist warmer
Early 20th century
Made in Palanga, Lithuania
6¼ x 2¾ in / 16 x 7 cm
LNM EMO 3042
Figure 30, page 162

23. Wrist warmers
Made in Palanga, Lithuania
5½ x 3¾ in / 14.2 x 9.5 cm
Palanga Traditional Textiles Education Center
Figure 31, page 163

24. Wrist warmers
Made in Palanga, Lithuania
Knitted in 2007 by Regina Andriekutė (born 1933)
6½ x 4 in / 16.7 x 10 cm
Palanga Traditional Textiles Education Center
Figure 32, page 163

25. Wrist warmers with button closure / *rankogaliai*
Late 19th to early 20th century
Made in Kalvarija, Žemaičiai County, in the region of Plungė, Lithuania
6 in / 15 cm long; 7½ and 8¾ in / 19 and 22 cm wide
ŽMA GEK 12.223 /a, b
Figure 33, page 164

26. Wrist warmers / *rankelkos*
Early 20th century
Made in Kelmė, Raseiniai County, Lithuania
6½ x 3¼ in / 16.5 x 8 cm
ŠAM EO 639/a, b
Figure 34, page 164

27. Wrist warmer / *rankauka*
Early 20th century
Made in the village of Graužai, Viduklė District, Raseiniai County, Lithuania
3½ x 3¼ in / 9 x 8.5 cm
ŠAM EO 625/1
Figure 35, page 164

28. Wrist warmers / *rankelkos*
Early 20th century
Made in the village of Graužai, Viduklė District, Raseiniai County, Lithuania
4¾ x 3¼ in / 12 x 8 cm
ŠAM EO 626/a, b
Figure 36, page 165

29. Wrist warmers / *rankelkos*
Early 20th century
Made in Paežeris, Nemakščiai District, Raseiniai County, Lithuania
4¼ x 4¼ in / 11 x 11 cm
ŠAM EO 622/a, b
Figure 27, page 167

30. Wrist warmers / *rankelkos*
Early 20th century
Made in Paežeris, Nemakščiai District, Raseiniai County, Lithuania
5 x 3½ in / 13 x 9 cm
ŠAM EO 629/a, b
Figure 28, page 166

31. Wrist warmer / *rankelka*
Early 20th century
Made in the village of Legotiškė, Nemakščiai District, Raseiniai County, Lithuania
5 x 3½ in / 13 x 9 cm
ŠAM EO 623
Figure 39, page 166

32. Wrist warmers / *rankelkos*
Early 20th century.
Made in the village of Legotiškė, Nemakščiai District, Raseiniai County, Lithuania
4¼ x 3¼ in / 11 x 8 cm
ŠAM EO 627
Figure 40, page 166

33. Wrist warmers / *rankovėlės, rankelkos*
Second half of 20th century
Made in Mosėdis, in the region of Skuodas, Lithuania
6¾ in / 17 cm long
ČDM E 4061/a, b
Figure 41, page 167

34. Wrist warmers / *rankovėlės, rankelkos*
Early 20th century
Made in Mosėdis, in the region of Skuodas, Lithuania
7½ in / 19 cm long
ČDM E 4062/a, b
Figure 42, page 167

35. Wrist warmer / *rankelka*
Early 20th century
Made in Šaukėnai, in the region of Kelmė, Lithuania
3¼ x 3½ in / 8 x 9 cm
ŠAM EO 630.
Figure 43, page 168

36. Wrist warmers / *rankelkos, rankoviečiai*
Early 20th century
From the village of Juodainiai, Laukuva County, in the region of Šilalė, Lithuania
5¾ x 4¼ in / 14.5 x 10.5 cm
ŠAM EO 634/a, b
Figure 44, page 168

37. Wrist warmers
Late 19th or early 20th century
Made in the village of Kanteniai, Nevarėnai County, in the region of Telšiai, Lithuania
6¾ x 3¼ in / 17 x 8.5 cm
LDM LA 1552/a, b
Figure 45, page 168

38. Wrist warmers / *rankelkos*
Early 20th century
Made in the village of Gilvyčiai, Skaudvilė District, Tauragė County, Lithuania
5 x 3½ in / 13 x 9 cm
ŠAM EO 624/a, b
Figure 46, page 169

39. Wrist warmers / *rankelkos*
Early 20th century
Made in the village of Gilvyčiai, Skaudvilė District, Tauragė County, Lithuania
4¼ x 3¼ in / 11 x 8 cm
ŠAM EO 640/a, b
Figure 47, page 169

| WRIST WARMERS FROM THE KLAIPEDA REGION |

A. With Beads

1. Wrist warmers / *maukos*
Made in Nemirseta, Klaipėda County, Lithuania
From "Lietuvininkų pirštinės" ("The Gloves of Lithuania Minor") by Irena Regina Merkienė and Marija Pautieniūtė–Banionienė. Lietuvos etnologija. (Lithuanian Ethnology) vol 3, Vilnius: Žara. 1998, pg. 191.
Project Illustrations 115 and 116.

B. Without Beads

2. Women's wrist warmers / *maukos*
Made in Lankupiai, in the region of Šilutė, Lithuania
4 x 2¾ in / 10 x 7 cm
LNM EMO 3041 /a, b
Figure 48, page 170

| WRIST WARMERS OF UNKNOWN ORIGIN |

A. With Beads

1. Wrist warmers / *rankelkos*
3¼ x 3¼ in / 8.5 x 8cm
ŠAM EO 457
Project Illustrations 117 and 118

2. Wrist warmers / *rankovička*
Early 20th century
2¼ x 2¾ in / 6 x 7 cm
ČDM E 1574
Project Illustrations 119 and 120

3. Wrist warmers / *runkaukos*
From *Lietuvių tautiniai drabužiai* (Lithuanian National Costume) by M. Glemžaitė. Vilnius. 1955, pg. 55.
Project Illustrations 121 and 122

4. Glove
National M.K. Čiurlionis Museum of Fine Arts
Project Illustrations 123 and 124

5. Wrist warmers
Origin unknown
3½ x 5 in / 9 x 13 cm
From the private collection of Lucija Dobrickienė
Project Illustrations 125 and 126

6. Gloves
PKM GEK 2719/E100
Project Illustrations 127 and 128

B. Without Beads

7. Wrist warmers / *rankelka*
Acquired by the museum in 1956
4¾ x 4¾ in / 12 x 12 cm
ŠAM EO 638
Figure 49, page 171

8. Linen wrist warmer / *rankelka*
Acquired by the museum in 1956
3½ x 3¼ in / 9 x 8 cm
ŠAM EO 636
Figure 50, page 171

9. Wrist warmer / *rankelka*
No data available. Private donation.
3¼ x 4 in / 8 x 10 cm
ŠAM EO 3007
Figure 51, page 171

Translator's Notes

It's been an honor to translate this book from Lithuanian into English so Irena Juškienė can share her passion for wrist warmers with a wider audience. I've added a little extra information to the knitting instructions to help English-speaking knitters. The following sections provide tips on pronouncing Lithuanian words, understanding the many Lithuanian words for "wrist warmer" in regional dialects, and understanding Lithuania's five regions and the organization of municipalities. Thank you to Sonata Eidikiene for reviewing and giving me feedback. Any mistakes that remain are my own.

Pronouncing Lithuanian Names and Words

I'm always asked how to pronounce Lithuanian words because, while it uses the Latin alphabet like English, there are different diacritical marks and sounds that are unique to Lithuanian. I can't provide a full lesson here, but these few tips may help you with the words and names in this book.

Consonants that are different from English:
c—ts as in cats
č—ch as in chicken
j—y as in yacht
š—sh as in sheep
r—rolled lightly (similar to Spanish)
ž—s as in pleasure

Vowels are also different from English, although the nuances are often difficult for English-speakers to hear. This is a basic list.
a, ą—as in car and father respectively
e, ę, ė—as in eat, man, and chair respectively
i—i as in sit
į and y—as in machine or as in meet
o—as in more
ų, ū—as in put and loot respectively

Synonyms for Wrist Warmers

In Lithuania, many different words were used to describe wrist warmers, just as in English they might be called wristers, mitts, fingerless gloves, cuffs, sweatbands, wristbands, wristlets, bangles, armlets, armbands, or even bracelets. These words are basically all synonyms, and mostly based on the Lithuanian words for hand (*ranka*) and wrist (*riešas*):
riešinės—wrist warmer
mankietai—cuffs
riešeliai—wristbands
rankovėlės—sleeves
rukavicos—gloves (Slavic)
rankafkos, rankapkos, rankaukos—hand "kerchiefs" or hand warmers
rankelkos—bangles or bracelets
rankovėčiai—arm cuffs
rukavičnikai—hand warmer
maukos—pipe(s) or tube(s)
rankogaliai—cuffs
zarankavkos—hand "kerchiefs" or hand warmers

Lithuanian Ethnographic Regions and National Costume

Although Lithuania is a small country compared to the United States, roughly the size of West Virginia, there are five distinct regions in the country which differ in geography, dialect, and style of dress.
Aukštaitija—Highlands, the northeast region
Dzūkija or *Dainava*—Land of Songs, the southeast region
Mažoji Lietuva—"Little Lithuania" or Lithuania Minor, the Klaipeda region, the western coastal region
Žemaitija—Lowlands, often called Samogitia in English-language publications, the northwest region
Suvalkija—the southwest region

The concept of a "Lithuanian national costume" was developed in the late nineteenth century and established in the early part of the twentieth century, as a way to promote Lithuanian nationality and ethnicity. This standardized folk costume was based on what could be learned about the holiday clothing worn by peasants or farmers. Each of the five regions in Lithuania has a distinct style of national costume.

Lithuanian Municipalities
There are many different names for municipalities and political entities in Lithuania. This is how I translated various terms used in this book. See footnote on page 187.
vnk. (vienkiemis)—farmstead
sen. (seniūnija)—neighborhood
k. (kaimas)—village
mstl. (miestelis)—town
ap. or apl. (apylinkė)—area or county, used in Soviet times
prp. (parapija)—parish
vls. (valsčius)—district
aps. (apskritis)—county
r. (rajonas)—region, used in Soviet times

Finishing Techniques

After your wrist warmers are knitted, seam the CO and BO edges together. Then, if desired, you can embellish the wrist edge with crochet or beaded trim.

Seaming Options

Mattress Stitch: With the right sides of the fabric facing up, place the two pieces to be seamed on a flat surface. Using a tapestry needle and matching yarn, catch the "v" just inside the edge of one piece of knitting. Repeat on the other piece. Continue to work from side to side, pulling gently on the yarn to close the seam after each stitch. The seam should be at the same tension as your knitting, and look like a row of knitting. Note that the V parts of the knit stitches are hidden between the ridges on garter stitch, so you'll have to stretch your knitting open a bit to find them.

Slip Stitch Crochet: Insert a crochet hook through the first stitch both layers of knitting and pull a loop of yarn through. Insert the crochet hook through the next stitch on both layers of knitting and pull a loop through both the knitting and the loop already on the hook. Repeat across to end of seam and fasten off.

If you prefer, you can begin your wrist warmers with a provisional cast on and join the seam with three-needle bind off, Russian grafting, or Kitchener stitch.

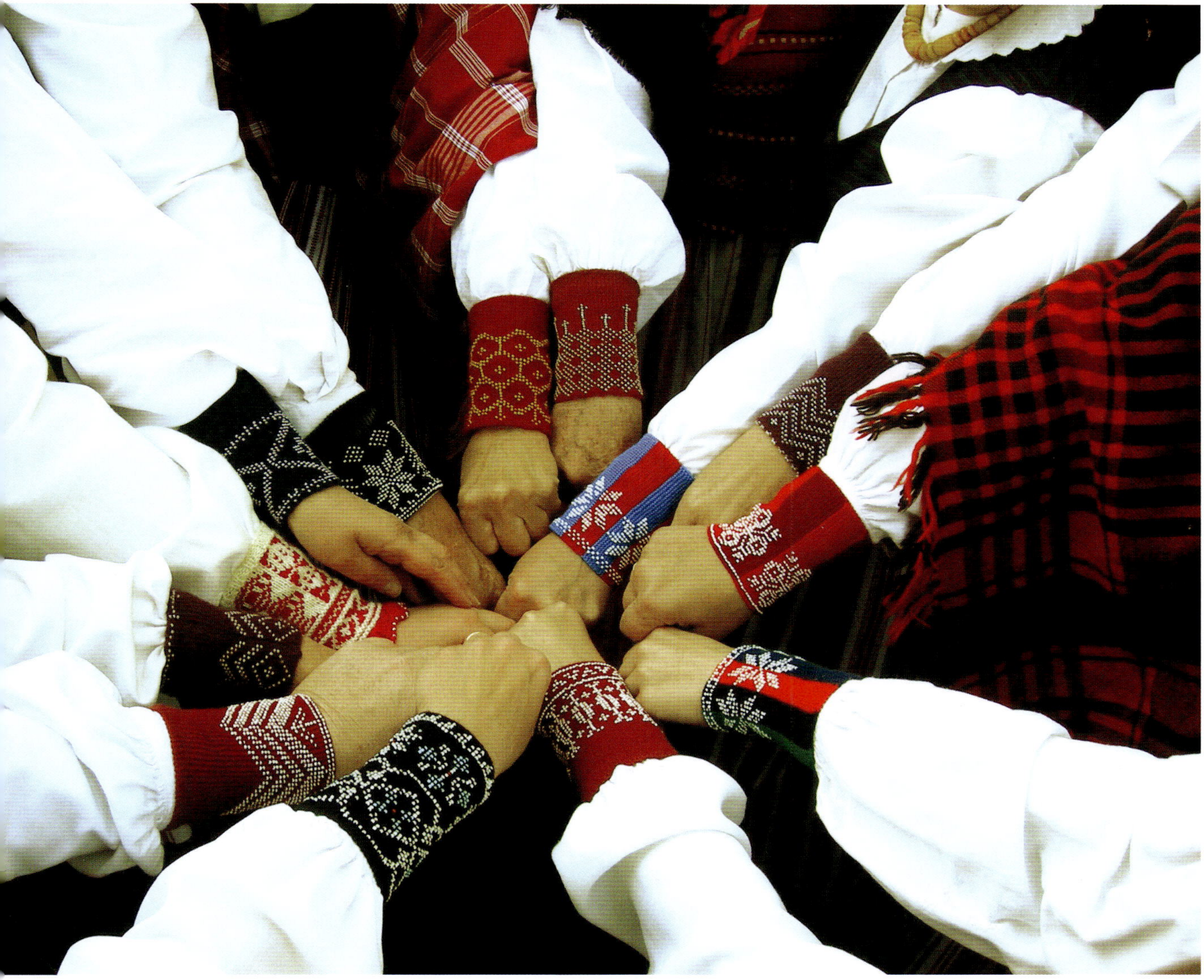

Crochet and Bead Trim Techniques

If desired, you can crochet a border on your wrist warmers, with or without incorporating additional beads into the design.

First, join the yarn to the knitting at one corner to work across one of the selvedge edges. With RS facing, insert a crochet hook into a stitch on the edge of the piece, and draw a loop through to the front. Wrap the yarn around the hook and draw a second loop through the first to secure.

Single Crochet: Working from right to left, insert the crochet hook into the next stitch on the edge of the piece. Pull the working yarn through to the front. Two loops are now on the hook. Pull the working yarn through both loops on the hook. One loop remains on the hook. Repeat until the entire edge is covered.

Crochet Shells: To be exact in your numbers, you'll need a multiple of 6 stitches plus 1. For example, 36 + 1 = 37 or 18 + 1 = 19. But since we are crocheting into the edge of a knitted piece, you can fudge on the last couple of shells to make them fit, if you need to. Join the yarn to the knitting (this counts as the first single crochet). *Skip 2 stitches, 5 double crochets into next stitch, skip next 2 stitches, single crochet into next stitch, repeat from * to end. Slip stitch to first single crochet to join and fasten off.

Crochet Picots: Work a row of single crochet, but after ever second, third, or fourth stitch (your choice) make a picot as follows: Chain 3, 4 or 5 stitches (again your choice), sl st to first stitch in the chain.

Beaded Picots: Attach the yarn as for other forms of crochet. Slide 5, 7 or 9 beads (your choice) up to the join, then make a single crochet. Pull the loop very large and draw the whole ball of yarn through it as if you're fastening off. Repeat all the way around and after the last stitch, cut the yarn and pull the tail through instead of the ball, to actually fasten off.

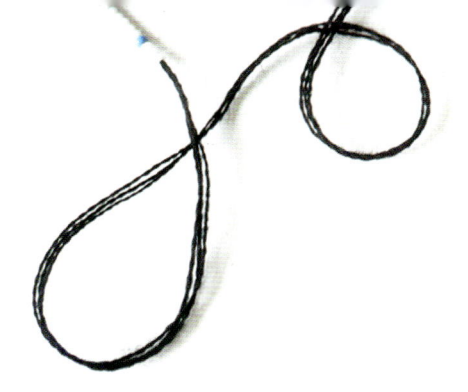

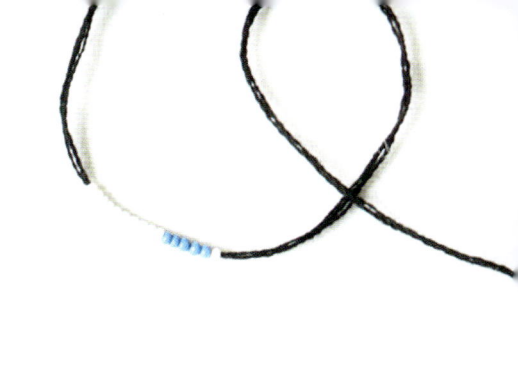

Yarn Information

In Lithuania, knitters today use a variety of wool yarns that are available locally. Light fingering weight or light sock yarn that is 100% wool or a wool/nylon blend will work well. Some yarns that are readily available in the USA and Europe include Cascade 220 Fingering, Brown Sheep Nature Spun Fingering, and Dale Garn Baby Ull. If you'd like to use a different yarn than those suggested here, remember: the yarn must be thin enough to string on seed beads in size 10/0 or size 8/0.

Seed beads are available from your local craft store, and from:

Michaels
www.michaels.com

Fire Mountain Gems and Beads
www.firemountaingems.com

The yarns listed above (and additional potential substitutes) are available from:

Cascade Yarns
www.cascadeyarns.com

Brown Sheep
www.brownsheep.com

Dale Garn
www.dalegarnnorthamerica.com

Webs—America's Yarn Store
75 Service Center Road
Northampton, MA 01060
800-367-9327
www.yarn.com

LoveKnitting.com
www.loveknitting.com/us

If you are unable to obtain any of the yarn used in this book, it can be replaced with a yarn of a similar weight and composition. Please note, however, the finished projects may vary slightly from those shown, depending on the yarn used. Try www.yarnsub.com for suggestions.

For more information on selecting or substituting yarn, contact your local yarn shop or an online store; they are familiar with all types of yarns and would be happy to help you. Additionally, the online knitting community at Ravelry.com has forums where you can post questions about specific yarns. Yarns come and go so quickly these days and there are so many beautiful yarns available.

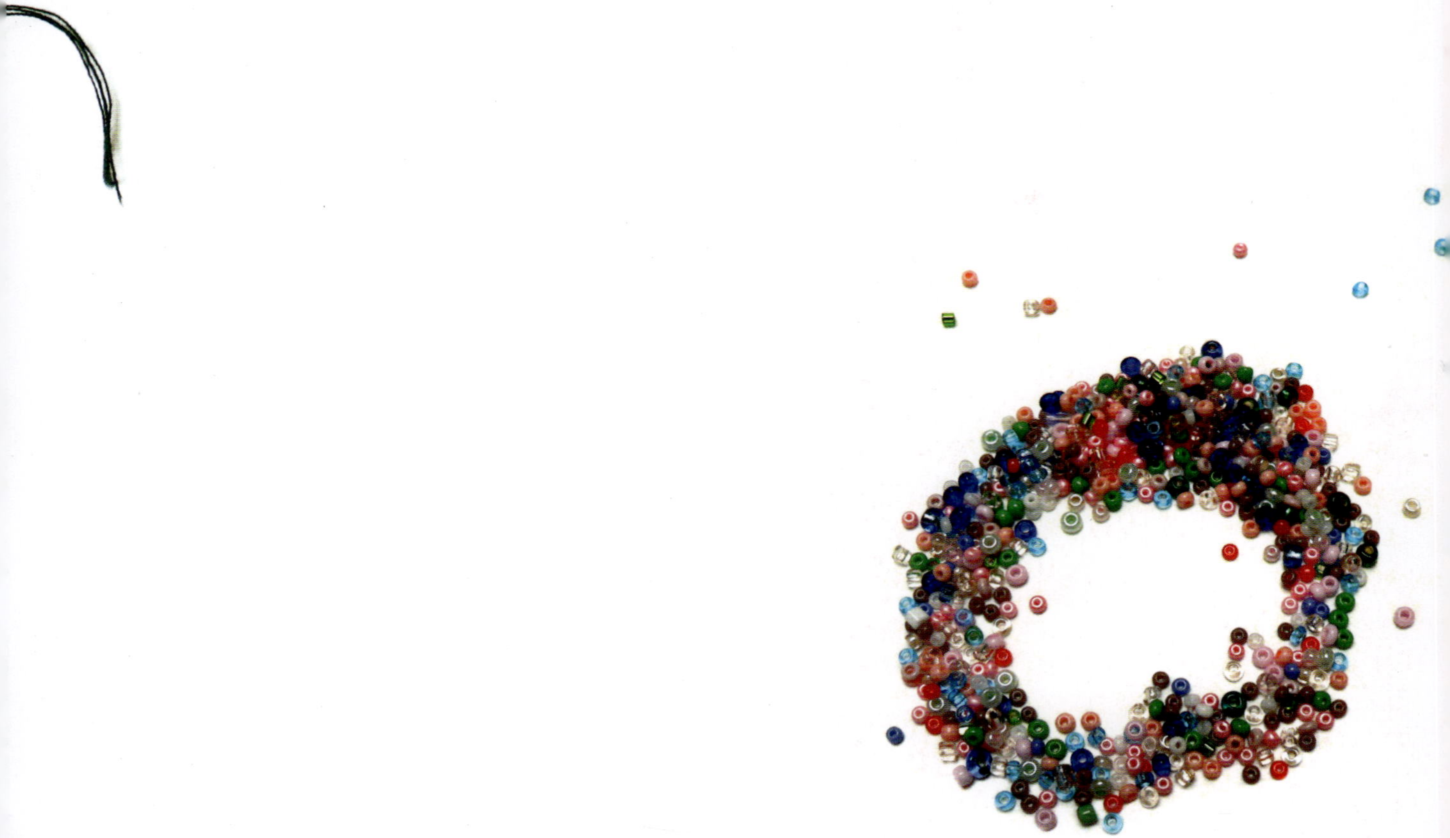